Sexual
BODY TALK

In a crowded room, a glance; a smile; a touch. Is this an exciting 'come-on' or just an over-friendly gesture? How can you tell? By using *sexual body talk.*

Whether we know it or not, we all send and receive sexual signals. Maybe these signals attract those we love, or those we want to love. Or maybe they give clear messages to others that sex is *not* on the agenda.

SEXUAL BODY TALK is the first book to explain how to understand, create and control these powerful sexual signals. In a lively and informative style, Susan Quilliam reveals ways you can use body talk to find a partner and develop a relationship, from first glances through to greater intimacy and love-making.

The early stages of a relationship are crucial. Mastering unspoken signals can greatly improve your chances. Chapter One reveals how to be in the right place at the right time, display yourself to advantage, use eye contact, make conversation and flirt with success. In Chapter Two, the emphasis is on moving to greater intimacy. Chapter Three focusses on the move to true sexuality. Learn how body talk can enhance sexual timing, mutual masturbation, love-making techniques and the pleasure of orgasm. And Chapter Four shows you how to build on a sexual relationship, using body talk to understand emotions and fantasies. By the end of this chapter, you will be ready to take your relationship into a lifelong love affair.

Lavishly illustrated throughout with color photographs and drawings, Susan Quilliam's brilliant insight into the non-verbal dance of attraction makes fascinating and essential reading. Follow her invaluable tips: your love life will never be the same again.

Sexual BODY TALK

SUSAN QUILLIAM

UNDERSTANDING
THE BODY LANGUAGE
OF ATTRACTION FROM
FIRST GLANCE TO
SEXUAL HAPPINESS

Carroll & Graf Publishers, Inc.
New York

First published in the United States in 1992
by Carroll & Graf Publishers, Inc.

Second printing 1994

Carroll & Graf Publishers, Inc.
260 Fifth Avenue
New York, NY 10001

Library of Congress Cataloging-in-Publication-Data

Quilliam, Susan
    Sexual body talk / by Susan Quilliam
        p.   cm.
    ISBN 0–88184–757–7 : $15.95
    1. Sex instruction.   2. Nonverbal communication (Psychology)
    I. Title
    HQ31.Q57   1992
    613.9′6—dc20   91–26194
                                                                  CIP

AN EDDISON · SADD EDITION
Edited, designed and produced by
Eddison Sadd Editions Limited
St Chad's Court
146B King's Cross Road
London WC1X 9DH

Phototypeset in Criterion Light by
Bookworm Typesetting, Manchester, England
Origination by Columbia Offset, Singapore
Produced by Mandarin Offset, Hong Kong
Printed and bound in Hong Kong

Frontispiece. In the first stages of love, everything is uncertain. He holds her to him, his arm encircling her waist, his hand clasping her shoulder; he is eager for intimacy. Perhaps, however, he is seeking a closeness that she is not quite ready for: her bent head and downcast eyes show some reticence. But we guess she will be happy to develop the relationship; her slight smile, her hand on his knee and the way her body rests easily against his all show increasing intimacy.

Opposite. As body talk brings us together, we begin to build a lifelong love. Founded on physical closeness and emotional harmony, it shows in every move we make. Here, they show delight in each other's company, hugging as close as they possibly can, entwining arms around bodies, rubbing noses, and entering into deep eye contact. Their smiles reflect their joy, their almost childlike expressions reflect their trust. This relationship is a lasting one, rooted in compatibility and love.

Overleaf. As we move emotionally closer to each other, our love finds expression through sex. With the removal of clothes comes intimacy and, if we can truly trust each other, an emotional as well as a physical abandonment to passion. Here, they cling tightly, lost in each other's touch, taste and smell; her hand grips his shoulder, their lips explore, their bodies move together. The rest of the world has ceased to exist as they create their own reality in love-making.

CONTENTS

Introducing Body Talk 8

INTRODUCING BODY TALK

In human relationships, it is never the words that really count. They are in the deepest sense unimportant, creating only 7 per cent of our communication. The other 93 per cent is body talk, the body language of posture, gesture and expression with which we communicate what we really mean.

In intimate relationships, we are inexorably drawn into using our bodies to communicate even more fully than usual. We move closer and converse through touch; we entwine tongues and communicate through taste; we listen and learn through the sound of heartbeat and of breathing. As lovers we grow to know each other more fully than ever before through an awareness of our own sexual body talk.

What you are reading is the first book aimed at increasing our knowledge and enjoyment of the non-verbal communication of intimate relationships. It has been written because, whilst we like to think of the language of love as being natural and spontaneous, we often fail to use it to its full potential. We may be nervous, for sex is so important that it cannot fail to be, at least occasionally, a source of anxiety. We may feel inhibited, for sex is so often an area in which we have been encouraged to deny our feelings and our sensitivities. And so much body talk happens at an unconscious level, with signals beyond both our awareness and our control, that we need to become conscious of them if we are to use them successfully.

This book exists to create new possibilities at all stages of a sexual relationship: at the beginning, when we are not close enough for words and rely entirely on body talk to make contact; during relationship development, when we are learning to adapt our sexuality to that of our partner and require ways to understand his or her needs and communicate our own; and during the continuation of a relationship, when

our sexual pleasure increasingly draws us into an emotional contact that is sometimes joyful but sometimes fraught. In all these situations, understanding what our own and our partner's body is saying will make all the difference to the way we give and receive love.

There are dangers in body talk. The belief that it tells us everything; the belief that it gives us power over others; the belief that it helps us to read minds: all these are fallacies. Be wary too about generalizing your interpretation of body-talk signals: a friendly touch in the wine bar at the end of the working day does not mean the same as that touch in the office, mid-morning. Equally, be aware that body talk can never tell you exactly what people are thinking; correctly used, however, it does accurately tell you what they are feeling, and so opens the door to a relationship that, both sexually and emotionally, is based on understanding and honesty.

If you really wish to become a partner who gives and receives pleasure unfailingly, then this book will show you how. It is not a sex manual. It does not list positions or suggest techniques. Instead it shows you in detail how to learn from your own and your partner's non-verbal communication, and to find out what sort of body talk works for you individually, in bed and out of it. Its explanations will tell you about body talk. Its pictures will show body talk in action. Its explorations will help you discover body talk. And, it will show you the skills and strategies of using body talk to form, create and build your sensual and sexual relationship. After that, it is up to you.

Body talk at its best. They are safe enough in each other's love to move close, reading each other's smiles as true signs of the emotion thèy feel. But they are communicating on many other levels, too: his firm touch on her arm confirms the message of commitment, while they are also unconsciously taking in the messages of smell, taste, heartbeat and breathing.

As with any language, sexual body talk has its letters of the alphabet, individual elements that we must know if we are to be literate. These elements recur throughout this book, signalling all kinds of emotion, sexual arousal and state of mind. Some elements we can alter by sheer force of will; others, like breathing and heart rate, we have no control over. Some can be read only by looking, others only by listening, and the more subtle ones by touching, tasting or smelling. By becoming aware of them in ourselves and by noticing them in our partner, we will soon become fluent.

Observing body talk from a distance or close-up, gives us numerous clues to our own or a loved one's true feelings. We can study posture: ways of standing, sitting or holding the body; movement and gesture patterns: ways of reacting, shifting or using hands and feet; and body tension: ways of holding muscles that betray stress or relaxation. We can note how the eyes, mouth and facial muscles work together to form a person's expressions. Once we know someone well, we may even chart the way skin colour changes with mood. Listening allows us to tune in to the sound of our own body or that of a potential partner. Voice – not the words used, but the way they are spoken – gives a sense of emphasis and mood. Listening to heart rate and breathing patterns gives vital signs about physical and emotional state.

When we reach out to make contact, we get further information, both from the response of a partner's skin as it moves under our fingers, and from the way a partner's body feels – warm, cold, hard, soft – as we touch it. Moving closer, when we get to know odour and taste, we have a further guide to emotions, charted by these intimate signals. It may take a while, some learning and practice, but all these elements of body talk will soon have meaning for us.

Right. The basics of body talk help us understand what is really happening here. His entire body leans in towards hers and his hand gesture is both affectionate and familiar; this is not the first time they have touched. Her smile returns his, but there is some uncertainty; her leg position turns the bottom half of her body away, and neither of her hands loosens its grasp on her wine glass to return his gesture. There may be some way to go before the promise of that touch is fulfilled.

Below. A warm and friendly smile seen in close-up allows us to notice minute details of physical appearance. The glimpse of teeth tells us that this is probably a woman's smile, as women are socially encouraged to smile more broadly and expressively than men. The raised corners of the lips and slight skin flush suggest the smile is genuine. We often fail to calibrate these minute physical signals as we see them in everyday life; and we will be even more unaware of our own signals.

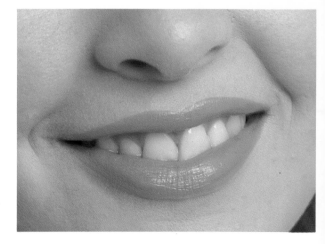

Above. The eye is a treasure-house of information as it can reveal whether someone is focussed externally or internally. External focus – looking interestedly at things, places and people – is shown in upright posture, outward movement and eye contact. When internally focussed, someone is considering their own responses, thoughts and emotions; it is shown by inward posture, a lack of movement and a defocussed or downward eye movement. Neither focus is good or bad; both can reveal feelings of contentment, or distress. But it is often vital to notice which focus a partner has so we can tell how to respond in the most loving way.

Left. The highly formal posture adopted by this young couple reveals that they are in the early stages of their relationship. There is substantial distance between them even though they are making contact: his hand folds over hers protectively, while her hand rests lightly and passively in his. Their direct eye contact, however, suggests that although they are at the stage of playing romantic roles, there is possibility for greater intimacy to develop later on.

Reading the non-verbal signals is vital if the early stages of a
relationship are to go well. Here, their body talk seems positive: the obvious
way their heads angle towards each other, his eye contact and her smile suggest
that they are enjoying each other's company. But he would do well to be aware of
her arm, twisted away and across her body as if to protect it. What is this
saying, and how can he encourage her to relax and trust him?

Chapter One
FIRST GLANCES

The first steps of a relationship are in many ways the most challenging, but also the most exciting. We have to take a risk, to approach or allow an approach, to show our feelings and accept others' confidences. But the sheer sense of possibility that accompanies these first steps makes it all worthwhile. Ahead may lie the relationship of a lifetime, pleasure and fulfilment we have never before suspected. Whatever happens, it is worth it. Yet when we enter any new interaction that we believe may end in love, all our prior experience suddenly seems irrelevant. However confident we are, we will worry about whether we are succeeding. How do we know what to do, where to look, how to speak? The vital importance of making the right impression overwhelms us and we often doubt we are making any impression at all. For nothing at this early stage can be clearly spoken, and everything has to go unsaid; only body talk can tell us what the other person is thinking and feeling, and the direction in which that person is moving, whether towards us or away.

And it is body talk too that supports us in the first process of 'checking out': gauging our own responses to other people and their reaction to us. We begin by noticing someone at a distance, move to holding eye contact, begin to talk, see each other closely, then touch. All the time we are checking whether we like this person and whether he or she likes us. At any point along the road we can withdraw, or be rejected. We may find that we have nothing in common and decide to go our separate ways at an early stage, or we may move more and more deeply into synchrony, until eventually our choice is made and we are on the brink of intimacy.

THE TIME, THE PLACE

Our potential for success in love begins not with us but with the context in which we find ourselves. The time and place in which we set our body-talk signals are what makes sense of them. In some situations, the possibilities for intimate contact are doomed; in others, they will immediately fulfil themselves.

Some settings clearly signal our availability for contact. In wine bars, discos, pubs or clubs, the expectation is for attraction. These places reflect their purpose in their decor: intimate tables for close conversations, low lighting for soft-focus gazing or rhythmic music to raise our heartbeat to passionate levels. In supermarkets, libraries or garages, however much we signal attraction, the message will take a while to get through. These settings have other purposes; love is clearly not on the agenda.

Equally, attraction signals are only read as such in a place that is safe. Emotional safety is high, for example, in the warmly supportive setting of a dinner party or wedding; physical safety is high when other people are around, though not in such a large crowd that any threat would go unnoticed. An approach that would be perfectly acceptable at a dinner party would, if made in a busy railway station or at a bus stop late at night, be highly threatening.

Finally, in some contexts, people are far too locked into their non-sexual personae to respond to us. At an important business meeting, sexual advances would be shocking; at the local nursery, parental roles may take up all our attention. However interested, people will only react when their sexual selves are uppermost.

True love settings, in short, can be found in those places where expectation, safety and our sexual selves combine. Once in such a setting, we only need opportunity – the possibility of meeting and making contact with others – to allow real body talk to begin.

Right. A holiday disco seems the perfect place and time. It is an atmospheric setting with a good gender balance and activity that allows us to move from person to person, checking out as we go. But romance is not in store for the trio we see pictured. He is obviously interested in the blonde girl, leaning forward, attempting to get eye contact, talking animatedly. But she is using every conceivable way to show lack of interest, blocking him off with leg, arm and negative eye contact. Her clothes signify that, in this context, her sexual self is on show; but in fact she feels neither safe nor inclined to respond. The dark girl, on the other hand, is so inclined. Her posture, which would seem relaxed in a domestic setting, is somehow overtly sexual in this situation, despite the fact that it is gaining no response.

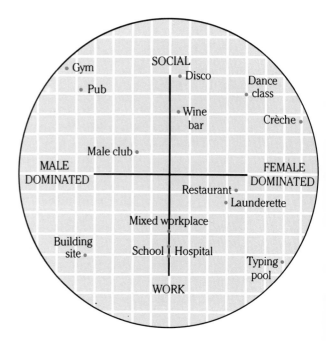

Left. The axes show two essential elements in choosing a setting for making the first approach. On the vertical axis, social settings always give more possibility than work ones because they contain social permission for love. Conversely, work settings are safer environments because we know that we will meet again tomorrow the person we fall for tonight. On the horizontal axis, any situation dominated by one gender totally loses safety because we either feel competitive with our own gender, or threatened by too many of the opposite sex. Perhaps the ideal for finding love is towards the top of the vertical axis, towards the centre of the horizontal axis. A social, mixed gender setting such as a disco or wine bar is the ideal.

Right. The top of the vertical axis shows structured settings, far more conducive to love if they facilitate mixing; in an unstructured situation we may not meet anyone, or may feel too emotionally unsafe to make the first move ourselves. Yet structured settings that militate against mixing can keep us away from the very people we wish to meet. On the horizontal axis, a crowded public place is right for the first moves in a pairing game as long as there is a reason to mix. For first contact we need to find a situation high on the vertical axis; but as we pair bond, we choose situations both more unstructured and more private, until the final act that needs to be played out alone.

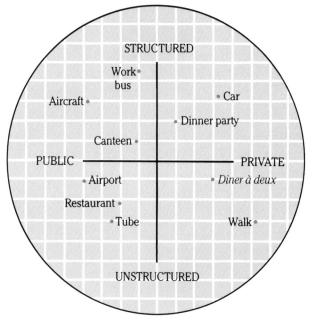

FIRST IMPRESSIONS

First impressions do count. The first four minutes of any meeting are sufficient for us to make a judgement about love potential. In this time, men tend to scan a woman's body completely, returning their gaze eventually to her face, while women concentrate on lips and eyes; we look for any elements to which we object, telling us that this person is not for us.

What do we look for with such an appearance inventory? Height may be important: women like their men taller than themselves, and men are wary of taller women, whom they often judge as ungainly or dominating. Slim is currently seen as

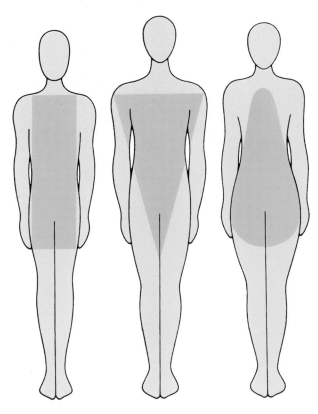

Psychologist W H Sheldon suggested three basic body types. The elegant ectomorph shape (*left*) was, he claimed, the sign of a quiet, stubborn, ambitious personality. The wide-shouldered mesomorph (*centre*) was adventurous and self-reliant. The pear-shaped endomorph (*right*) indicated a warm, talkative and trusting temperament.

beautiful for both sexes. Men often think that women prefer big muscles and broad shoulders but women questioned for a recent study preferred slim men with small hips.

Dress will also influence; we believe that outside reflects inside, and that unfashionable clothes, for example, mean a staid, probably unsexual personality, and that padded 'power' shoulders indicate a high achiever. Colouring counts; the majority of us will choose partners from within our own racial group, though more of us cross the cultural divide now than did even ten years ago. Blondes are seen to have more fun, and a blonde woman will receive a stronger response than a brunette even when, as in a recent experiment, it is the same girl in a wig!

Equally, we judge others on facial expression; we check features against some complex mental check-list of our own to find out if what we see is attractive to us. If eyes are too small or mouth too wide, then interest is lost. We move on.

How do we make these arbitrary judgements? We are influenced firstly by cultural or media stereotypes, the images we are fed about what currently is or is not attractive. We also tend to favour people who emphasize gender signals, such as breasts, lips, buttocks or eyes. We believe too that appearance shows personality, so reject people because we believe their thin lips mean they are stingy or their make-up means they are flighty. Our own personal memories also affect our judgement; bad experiences with blond men, for example, will bias us against them.

Many of our judgements about appearance are falsely based. Media stereotypes are the product of an advertising executive's imagination; personality theories are often a legacy of medieval superstition; and past traumas with blond men do not mean that all such men spell disaster. But we cannot help ourselves. We still judge our love possibilities on first impressions.

Below. You might think that her coloured hair, heavy make-up and black leather gear would indicate sexual wildness; but in fact her still posture and downcast eyes contradict this myth.

Below. Dark hair and beard are seen traditionally as powerful, masculine images. His closed posture and direct gaze also create the impression that he is dominant and assertive.

Below. The classic female beauty: slim, tall and blonde. Her high-necked elegance, impeccable make-up, sunglasses and composed appearance give a 'touch-me-not' air.

Right. Classic good looks and the smile reaching eyes and mouth attract at once. The current fashion for a clean-shaven face or designer stubble indicates male attempts to hint at their more feminine, sensitive side.

Left. Signs of ageing and increased weight are often thought to make a woman less beautiful, but it is the overall impression that counts, and other factors must be taken into consideration. Here, her humorous glance and confident posture will attract. Short hair in a woman suggests someone active and energetic, while long hair is often perceived as an indication of sensuality.

Left. His relaxed posture, smile and casual clothes give an impression of an easy-going personality. He displays signs of ageing, which are said to indicate less sexual stamina, but many would argue that appearances are very deceptive!

AVAILABLE OR NOT?

Who is available and who is not? We need, at the start of any relationship, to gauge whether it is worth going ahead, so the first decision we make when considering an approach is whether it will be welcomed.

In making that decision, ambiguity always hinders us. Though many Eastern cultures dictate changes of dress, hair or jewellery to signal the transition to a married state, we have few clear signs of availability status in Western society. Even wearing a wedding ring may be misleading, indicating a past marriage or a need for emotional security; not wearing one certainly does not mean availability, especially for men.

Availability signals also differ from gender to gender causing untold misunderstanding. To her, availability is signalled by behaviour: interest in the other person, subtle eye and body contact, smiles and questions. To him, availability is signalled less by interaction than by overt sexual display: if breasts are on show he may assume, not unnaturally, that they are displayed for a reason. But to a woman, dress and make-up are to enhance, not to signal interest. Firstly, she has little choice; in Western society, a woman is supposed to dress attractively whatever her availability status. If she dresses attractively, she usually dresses fashionably, and if she dresses fashionably, she often dresses sexually. She often has no choice for the whole female fashion industry is set up to create images of sexual attraction. If she wears a mini-skirt, she will show her legs, thereby sending out certain messages to men, irrespective of whether she is single, married, a nymphomaniac or a virgin.

Secondly, a woman rarely dresses to signal her general need for a mate. A very young woman will dress sexily to gain attention, though she may soon find that the attention she gets is more than she wants. She quickly learns to be more choosy, to decide whom she will attract

Above. Is this woman available or not? Ignore her short skirt, which is just a red herring. She is not using any of the more overt signs of availability. For a woman of her age alone in a public situation, they would be just too obvious and she would almost certainly get approached by someone believing she only wanted sex. Look, however, at the way she is angled into the room. Her body is set away from the bar, shoulders and hips turned so that she can be seen, yet straight backed so that she looks certain of what she is doing. Her posture and slight smile are graceful enough to be attractive, yet not so sexual that she seems threatening; if anything, she looks demure. But all her behaviour is externally orientated. She looks directly outwards and downwards, not challengingly assertive as she gazes around the room, but waiting to be noticed and to make first eye contact. When all these factors are considered, it is obvious by the way she is sitting that she has, in fact, nothing to do but to wait for someone to come and talk to her.

Above. What a difference one shift in posture makes. Now, all the signals are negative. The same woman, dressed in the same way at the same bar, is patently unavailable. With only a slight alteration, she has changed the whole message and it is clear that anyone who tried to approach her would get short shrift. What has she done? By turning slightly back to the bar, she has altered her direction, no longer making the room her focus of attention. She is completely internally orientated. Her head has dropped slightly to concentrate her attention and her eye contact on her fingers, which are entwined in a way that indicates a strong and involving emotion; this woman clearly has something on her mind. Her raised right shoulder gives an unbalanced, unhappy look to her position, echoed by tension lines around her mouth and eyes and nerves standing out on her throat. She is not only signalling no by failing to look around the room to try and make eye contact; she is also signalling that other things concern her far more than a possible pick-up.

and then focus in with body-talk signals, encouraging with eyes, words and touch; if not interested, she simply reverts to behaviour more friendly than sexual. Usually – and often to men's confusion – she reserves her more risqué outfits for after she has found a partner, when she is confident that she has 'protection' when she chooses to wear them.

For a man, things are different. Even in this day and age he is the prime mover in making contact and thus has a lot more at stake. He has to judge very quickly what the situation is. His status as initiator also means that society gives him few dress signals with which to show his availability; whether he is a wolf or a baa-lamb, on the prowl or happily pair-bonded, he will still wear clothes within the same narrow range. If he dresses fashionably, this signals only that he knows about fashion; if he dresses unawarely, this may communicate a lack of self-esteem but it says nothing about his need for a partner. When very young, he may signal interest primarily by making a move, often rushing the slow dance to intimacy and hence frequently getting rejected. He may be tempted to believe in the significance of overt signals, of dress and make-up, and may again, for reasons explained above, be disappointed. Or he may show interest by displaying his talents, talking proudly about them, seeking to impress her in conversation or by extrovert behaviour. But all too often she will code his interest as showing off, his attempts to impress as simply masculine ego; she rarely sees them as the signals they really are, of wanting to be noticed or seen to be available.

Yet if he learns that availability and interest are signalled by eye contact, smiles, movements towards the other person and concerned questions, then he will suddenly, and to his amazement, find that his interest is returned and that his intentions are being understood.

DISPLAYING TO ADVANTAGE

When we see someone we want to attract, we do what all the animals do: we show ourselves off to best advantage. Like the peacock, we flutter our plumes and display our attractions. Preening and displaying behaviour is vital, not only because it makes us look desirable, but also because it signals to the other person that we are interested, an irresistible message.

When we preen, we use all our body-talk skills to improve our appearance. We may pat our hair into place, lick our lips to make them inviting, straighten our back and pull in our stomach. Women will unconsciously adjust a belt, skirt length or earrings; men will straighten their tie or stroke their chin as if to smooth away a beard.

Once groomed, we are then ready to display, making slightly exaggerated movements that show off our attractions at a distance. This may be a personal display of our strongest points (shiny hair, long legs, best side) or a display of those elements of our appearance that are most masculine or feminine. Women may sit up and straighten their back to show their breasts, men may angle themselves to make shoulders appear bigger and buttocks smaller. We may even go so far as to unconsciously indicate our sexual parts, smoothing hands over breasts or pouting our lips. We will also touch ourselves far more than normal to remind whoever is watching of the delights of touching, particularly the delights of touching us.

As well as a gender display, we will probably also opt for a display of personality. For preening and displaying are not only about sexual invitation; we are nearly always also inviting the other person to enter a relationship with us, a relationship where who we are is as important as what we are like in bed. So we will smile and laugh to show that we have a sense of humour. We will look serious to indicate that we should be taken seriously. A woman may adopt a

Below. An ideal way to display her attractive legs. She shows them off to even greater advantage by lifting one slightly so that the shape shows more clearly, and by pointing her toe. Here the short skirt sets off the display, although in some situations displaying by hiding features – by lace at the neck, or a shawl across the shoulders – can be even more effective.

EXPLORATION
Is someone trying to impress you? If you are unsure, see how many of these examples of display behaviour you can spot:
- Preening
- Personal display
- Gender display
- Sexual display
- Personality display
- Directional pointers
- Interest display

Left. Even when you are on talking terms, displaying is a way of signalling interest. She angles her body, weight on one leg, and her uplifted head and winning smile give a 'little girl' image that she knows is hard to resist. His centred position and angled elbow create a gender display of his height and broad shoulders, while the listening position of his head shows he cares. Display behaviour is always externally focussed; an obvious awareness of the other person looking at us is one of the ways we signal that he or she is special.

head-on-one-side stance to seem sympathetic and supportive. A man may stand more erect to appear confident.

The final type of display, used once we are sure that we have been noticed and that our attention is returned, is one of interest. This signals, 'yes, it is you I am aiming at,' and involves postural and gestural pointers: feet, head or hands aligned in the direction of the potential partner. Even across a room, these pointers are noticeable by the person at whom they are aimed.

There are dangers to displaying; overdone, it can signal an easy availability that can lose you the partner you want. It can also gain you a partner you do not want who fails to realize that your efforts are aimed at someone else. But displaying well done is a wonderful, effective and fun way in which to flutter our tail feathers and to attract a mate.

21

KEEP YOUR DISTANCE

How far is a new relationship progressing? To find out, look at the distance between you. Ancient survival instincts mean that we mark out territory as ours, allowing strangers to approach only so far as we trust and like them. The closer we let people get, the more they can tell about us, reading more from the face, hearing more in voice tone, eventually even sensing mood from smell and taste. Allowing someone very close is a sign of extremely high emotional trust.

There are four zones of distance within which we operate. The public zone, from over 12 feet away, allows us to see but not clearly hear someone; we pass people on the street this far away. The social zone, from 12 feet to 4 feet, allows us to hear conversation and pick up visual detail but not touch; most colleagues and acquaintances come this close. In the personal zone, from 4 feet to 1½ feet, friends are allowed to see and hear us accurately, and reach out and touch us. In the final, intimate zone of below 1½ feet, we allow only children, close friends and lovers. At this distance, our sight loses focus as we stare, our voice drops lower and we can smell and sense body heat. It is easy to touch.

These distances are not fixed. They tend to reduce between two women and extend between two men. They vary between cultures: British and Scandinavians guard their distance zones, while comfortable social distances for some Mediterranean and African cultures are considerably closer than the ones outlined above.

But in all cases, if the agreed, often unconscious distance is breeched without invitation, then everyone starts to feel uncomfortable, even threatened. In public places such as crowded trains, where such breeching is unavoidable, we protect ourselves by putting up personal barriers: focussing internally, crossing our arms over our chest and sitting very still.

When someone approaches closer than we want in a private situation, we may react more strongly. Our barriers may be bags, books, crossed arms or stuck-out legs; turning away or losing eye contact; pointing out something that will take attention away from us: anything in order to extend the distance and so reduce the emotional pressure. This happens even in established, intimate relationships when we feel we want to be emotionally private and protect our personal space avidly.

What, though, if our intentions are totally opposite? What if rather than protecting, we want to bridge the distance between ourselves and a potential partner? The first move, from a public distance, is to indicate interest by displaying (see pages 20–21) and then by eye contact (see pages 24–25). But having confirmed that a move into social distance would be welcomed, there still needs to be an acceptable reason to cross the divide. Now is the time to use distance excusers, such as asking for a light, sharing an umbrella or dancing together, all socially acceptable ways to make the move, while parties and discos reduce distance simply by being crowded. Uncrowded social situations often feel disappointing because they provide no opportunity literally to diminish distance, and so give less opportunity for emotional closeness.

The final move into intimate distance may occur both suddenly and rapidly; once the decision is made by both of us, it may take only seconds for eyes to meet and for us then to move close to each other. Once that happens, and intimate distance is breeched, then the chances of subsequent sexual contact increase ten-fold. So in many ways, that move is a make-or-break situation. If we attempt it and fail, then we may jolt a potential partner into terminal defensiveness. If we succeed, then simply by making the move into intimate space, we may create an intimate relationship.

Left. It just would not be acceptable for this couple, who have obviously never met before, to stand close enough to touch. But they do the next-best thing. They stand in the same doorway and whilst keeping a respectable, safe social distance by moving to the extreme end of the space available, they begin to bridge the gap. They stand in the same way, they take the same posture, holding their respective briefcases in the same hand. They share a common goal, perhaps waiting for a bus or waiting for a business contact. And any minute now, she will take his hint and ask him whether that really is the time.

EXPLORATION

How far do you let people into your life? The diagram (*below*) shows the four distance zones: (1) public, over 12 feet; (2) social, from 12 feet to 4 feet; (3) personal, from 4 feet to 1½ feet and (4) intimate, below 1½ feet. Choose four people you know to different degrees, such as an acquaintance, a colleague, a friend and a partner. How near do you think you could let them approach you whilst still feeling comfortable? Next time you meet them, experiment with moving closer and further away, testing just where your actual distance-comfort zones are in each instance. How close could you be in theory, and how close could you be in practice?

1   2   3   4

THE LOOK OF LOVE

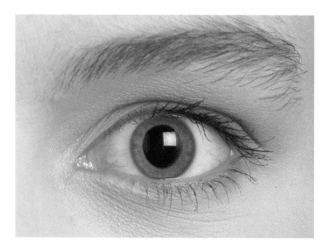

Above. Pupil dilation can be seen even from a distance, the centre of the iris widening to allow more light to enter. Such dilation suggests responsiveness and receptivity; it may not be an attractive feature in itself, but it flatters a potential partner that he or she is an object of interest. In olden days, Italian courtesans used minute quantities of the poison belladonna to dilate their pupils as a beauty aid. Blue eyes show pupil dilation clearly, and this may be why they are seen as so attractive.

Eyes are our windows on the world; as babies, we can hold eye contact with our mother as early as four weeks old. As we grow, we use our eyes to signal not only our interest in things, but also our physical, mental and emotional states. When we fall in love, our eye signals, unconscious and uncontrollable, are an undeniable statement of what we are feeling.

Eyes make it easy to signal or to notice initial attraction when the public distance zone has yet to be crossed, because the whites of the eyes show the direction in which someone is looking. After this first awareness, eye-contact games are fun to play. When at a distance, we can prolong a mutual stare far beyond what would normally be acceptable; or we can look steadily, glance away, then look back quickly to catch the other's unguarded gaze.

When such contact has been made, the rules change. When we are close to someone, it is easy to spot subtle signals of disinterest, so we tend to be more wary of what we reveal through our glances and to respect the other person's privacy by not holding his or her gaze too much. Meanwhile, however, we will continue to judge intentions through what the eyes reveal.

The length of time spent looking at another person indicates both interest and confidence. Men will often look longer and more overtly than women; and a prolonged stare by a woman is generally interpreted as threatening or as an overt sexual invitation. On the other hand, men will also look away for longer: this is a signal of dominance in our society. Women tend to glance away and back more often at someone in whom they are interested, showing by their constant checking out that other people's welfare and happiness are important to them.

The direction in which eyes are looking can indicate feelings a partner is having: research has

Left. His direct stare shows that he is interested in what she is saying. As she looks away to grasp her thought, focussing internally for just a moment, she is also flirting with him, using the break in eye contact both to keep his interest rising and to show hers. Her smile and the angle of her head reassure him that the loss of eye contact does not mean loss of interest.

Above. Her clear gaze shows she is content. The slight muscle tension around her eyes comes from focussing, and from muscle tone given to her whole face by the smile we guess is on her lips.

Above. Unsure eyes are revealed by the muscle tension around lids and brows. The 'puzzled' lines at the centre of her forehead show she is coming to some decision.

shown that a prolonged downwards glance often reflects strong inner emotion; an upwards glance indicates that we have a mental image; while a sideways look can mean that we are rehearsing or remembering words or sounds.

The shape of eyes as they gaze is also significant. Wide eyes, particularly when accompanied by pupil dilation, show interest. Narrowed ones can indicate either desire as we focus our gaze on to the person we want, or uncertainty as we check out mentally and with furrowed brow what the alternatives are. Moisture around the eyes is a sure signal of emotional arousal; a knowledgeable lover will be able to spot in a partner the filmy glaze of passion or the subtle rise of wetness along the lower lid that is the precursor of tears.

And when we do finally fall, the prolonged, direct, slightly defocused stare into our partner's eyes is unmistakeable: the look of love.

Above. A wide, penetrating stare gives angry eyes their impact. Slight reddening around the upper and lower lids indicates strong emotion; tears of anger may be on the way.

SPEAK TO ME

S exual body talk is not about the words people say. Nevertheless, we learn a great deal about potential partners from the way they speak. Voice is initially a key influence on our response, particularly if it is the primary way we make contact, as in a phone call.

We often judge personality by volume of voice: soft, low voices may indicate shyness or introversion, while loud ones suggest a confident, assertive individual. But volume also differs with culture and context: American and Mediterranean speakers often talk more loudly than British ones, while most of us will talk softly in a library, for example, and raise the volume when out of doors.

We tend to associate speed and rhythm of voice with thought patterns, judging quick speakers to be quick thinkers and vice versa. Yet excitement will quicken a partner's natural voice speed, while sadness or depression will slow it, and natural voice rhythm may be interrupted by the emphasizing of certain words or phrases that are important to the speaker.

Pitch is a classic, though mythical, indicator of masculinity in males and femininity in females. We imagine that well-built men will have deep voices and feminine women will have high-pitched ones. In fact, the range overlaps a great deal and huskiness in voice tone is often thought to be particularly attractive for women. Breathiness of speech, on the other hand, may be seen as showing a placating or unassertive personality, though most people will assume a breathless voice tone when under strain.

There are signals other than auditory ones that give us information when we talk. A whole range of hand and body movements often accompanies speech, emphasizing, clarifying and giving extra meaning to each word. These 'baton' gestures beat out the rhythm of a sentence with hands or feet, underlining what is truly important to the speaker. We may use, or see, 'proximal' inward movements, showing the speaker is anxious and needs support; or we may note 'distal' outward movements, showing the speaker including others.

Once our first impressions have been established, we often show our feelings more clearly in voice than in behaviour, which we more consciously guard. For when we are attracted to someone, our voice alters. It spontaneously lowers in tone and volume, becoming deeper and slower, encouraging the other person to come closer in order to hear. Expert seducers use this voice modulation gradually to move a hitherto non-intimate conversation slowly and subtly in the direction they want it to go.

Equally, two people who are becoming emotionally involved not only learn to match each other's voice tone (*see* pages 32–33) but also to pick up the natural rhythm of equal conversa-

There is no rapport here. Their statements are totally unlinked; they hardly hear what the other is saying.

He thinks he is doing well because he is talking a lot. She is asking the questions and working out how fast she can escape.

She is interested, largely encouraged by his genuine questions. The relationship is unbalanced, but they have a chance.

This relationship will definitely last. Both are contributing equally, asking, answering and volunteering information.

Above. The girls on the left are having a relaxed but equal conversation. This is shown in the way that they are turned towards each other, while they parallel expression and hand movements. In the centre, however, a very different interaction is taking place. His animated face and wide hand gestures show he is deeply involved in the topic he is talking about, but she has withdrawn from the conversation and focussed internally, letting her eyes drop and setting her face in a polite smile.

Above. If you really want to spot whether a relationship will be successful, then notice the balance of verbal interaction. Conversation can be divided into statements (S), questions (Q) and answers (A). The four diagrams show typical interactions that reveal much about the relationship of the speakers. The more equally each person contributes in each of these modes, and in a way that links in to what has just been said, the more chance the relationship has of lasting.

tion. We sense when it is time to speak and when it is time to listen. We sense when a partner wants to speak by noticing 'interrupt cues', such as overlapping speech, 'yes but' phrases and attention-getting baton gestures. We learn when the other has finished speaking by checking their 'turn-yielding' cues, such as emphasizing a phrase that obviously ends a sentence, taking up eye contact again when handing over control and giving a final baton gesture to indicate the completion of a turn.

The real sign of a developing relationship is the growing ability to listen and learn.

EXPLORATION
Next time you are in conversation with someone, tune out from the words themselves and tune in to the non-verbal signals. What are these signals telling you about what the other person is saying?
- Volume of speech: how loud, what variations?
- Speed: how quickly are words spoken, what variations?
- Rhythm: what rhythms can you spot, what variations?
- Pitch: is the voice high or low, what variations?
- Baton gestures: what do they emphasize?
- Proximal or distal movements: which are they?
- Interrupt and turn-yielding signals: what are they?

THE FINE ART OF FLIRTING

Flirting is a fine art. At its lightest, it is used to lead people on when we have no intention of following through to a serious relationship. More sincerely used, it is a way of overtly showing that we are interested in someone and keeping that person interested in us at the same time.

Flirting has three components: the 'come-on', the 'pull-back' and the 'block-off'. All are carefully designed to keep us and a potential partner in contact at the very early stages of a relationship, until we have both decided to take it further or made the decision that further is not where we want to go.

The 'come-on' consists of all the complex signals of attraction, magnified and exaggerated. We move closer, we face directly, we keep eye contact, we display, we preen, we focus externally, we make our partner the centre of attention. Our voice drops low and becomes soft and husky, mimicking the tones it may take when love-making. We find reasons – excuses even – for light touches, as we pour her wine, pass something from hand to hand or pat his arm at the climax of a joke.

We also smile, the genuine smile that is broad and symmetrical, that raises the corners of the mouth and goes right up to create wrinkles round the eyes. Men smile less than women but, when flirting, still smile a great deal.

All these components of the come-on phase are designed to reassure our potential partner that, even though the two of us are now close, we have not lost interest. If anything, we are more enamoured. But true flirting means adding an extra dimension at this stage, in case the other party starts relaxing or looking elsewhere, even in the brief time we have known each other.

This dimension is the 'pull-back': minute and momentary turning-away gestures or angled movements. We tilt our head sideways, glance off in another direction, let eye contact slide just for

a moment and then return. We hide ourselves – behind a fan was the Victorian equivalent – with a wine glass, a hand raised to our face or mouth, or behind softly lowered eyelashes.

In this pull-back phase, which may last just a few seconds but is repeated regularly at very short intervals, our voice goes back to its normal state, almost as if we have had second thoughts about intimacy. We pull back mentally too, and take on an internal focus, maybe gazing off into the distance or closing our eyes briefly as if needing a break from contact. The whole impression is one of momentary withdrawal.

Above. She blocks him off both physically and emotionally. Her hand at his lapel means that they are obviously linked physically, a sign to others not to intrude; the touch also acts to keep his attention on her. She keeps his attention emotionally, too; it is obvious she is saying something serious as her tense mouth and downcast eyes give all the signals. He has to respond by turning inwards to her, and her expression is a deterrent to anyone else from joining the interaction.

Left. Gentle flirting over a menu. While glancing sideways, her head is tilted to one side, her body angled away from him but her legs crossed towards him. Meanwhile, he is briefly pulling back. The menu gives him an excuse for momentarily turning his attention elsewhere and losing eye contact with her. But he maintains interest by leaning in towards her and by accepting her invitation to touch her hand.

Above. He blocks her off with his arm across the side of her chair, his shoulder also keeping her shielded from making eye contact with anyone but him. This is a typically male block-off, where the arm or leg is stretched out to make it difficult for any other males to approach or for her to escape. In this case, she obviously has no wish to; she in turn is blocking him off from outside contact by keeping him locked in eye contact and laughter. Notice too her 'hiding' come-on, as she shields her face with one hand.

EXPLORATION
Think of a time when you flirted with someone. What did you do that got you what you wanted? What could you have done that would have made your flirting more successful that time?

And we smile less, and less widely: narrow smiles, not showing our teeth, almost formal in their amusement, suggesting that we are suddenly aware of more serious emotion.

But all this pulling-back, designed to keep the other person interested, may in fact have a danger: that in the few brief seconds we are pulling back our potential partner may lose interest and emotionally leave us. Our solution is to create a block, preventing our partner both from noticing someone else and from being noticed by other people. We do this in a number of ways. Perhaps we use our body strategically,

leaning over or placing an arm or leg across our partner's path. A movement, a word, or a touch can all be employed to focus attention on ourselves.

Such flirting can confuse if you are on the receiving end. It can be seen as sexual teasing and gets some people very angry. It also makes it difficult to tell whether or not someone is really interested. The acid test – when your partner is in the pull-back phase – is whether you are being blocked off from other contacts at the same time. If so, you are undoubtedly experiencing flirting, not deserting, behaviour.

Left. He moves in close to hold and touch but she is obviously in a very different mood. She wants to keep him away. Her body turns away as far as possible, while her head is angled from him. One hand, trapped between them, hangs loosely, while the other hand moves across in a spontaneous gesture to protect her breasts. Her eyes are down so she cannot meet his gaze, and her set mouth also tells us that she has nothing more to say to him. Perhaps this is, however, only a stage in their relationship. Often such a withdrawal is simply a chance to pull back for a while at the start of a relationship and slow the pace down. If so, then you can help a potential partner think through what he or she really wants by easing up on closeness signals. For a while, increase the natural distance between you, moving back from the intimate to the personal zone. Hold back from touching and closing in, aiming instead to mirror your partner's posture. Keep eye contact down and raise your voice to a less intimate level. It could be that, given the extra space that this body talk allows, a potential partner will feel able to breathe again, and then to move forward slowly to further intimacy.

SAYING NO

When in love, 'no' can sometimes mean 'yes'. The flirting pull-back really means 'come and get me'; but sometimes no really does mean no, whether a person has the courage to say it straight out, or has to signal it in more subtle ways. How do we tell when what we are seeing – or giving – is a genuine no, a pull-back from further intimacy or a clear statement to go away?

Reservations or misgivings are often directly signalled. People who tell us no with clear eye contact, their body straight and square and an even, balanced voice tone have to be taken seriously. They mean it. And if we want others to know that we mean it too, we can adopt this body talk when we face them.

All too often, however, such a clear no is hard to give; it is difficult, even at the start of the relationship, to reject a partner directly. We will often use or receive part rejections, pull-backs from anything further. Notice a turned-away posture, a blocking gesture by placing arms across the chest or a knees-together position. There is little body movement, a heaviness and tiredness that carries through to the voice; alternatively, there is a nervous voice tone and lots of false starts to sentences, hesitation or swallowed words. Even if we are clear that no is the message, we are often afraid to say it.

There will be noticeable tension, exacerbated by shallow, irregular breathing. If touched, hands may be cold or clammy though, despite this, there will be a lot of self-touching, seeking comfort by rubbing cheek, hand or mouth.

Even if we say no quite quickly, we will pay little attention to what is happening externally, such as how a partner is reacting, and avoid face-to-face or eye-to-eye contact. Instead we will fidget, or our internally focussed attention will constantly move away to other things, as if we wished we were somewhere else.

How can you handle such a rejection if you are on the receiving end? If it is genuine – seeming very different from the flirting pull-back – then there is only one way: acceptance. If in doubt, retreat gracefully.

Perhaps you feel that the rejection is not the complete story, however, that there may be a chance to try again. If this is so, then face the other person squarely, and keep eye contact as you ask directly whether he or she wants to take things further. If the answer is really yes, your partner should now be able to tell you so or, if it is not, then thus challenged, may feel able to tell you the truth.

Above. When saying no, we may feel we have to soften our refusal; this is particularly true for women, who are brought up to need approval. Her smile is partly genuine, as she wants to please, but still irregular enough to fall short of a true smile. Her eyes contradict the smiling message, their wary look showing her mixed feelings.

EXPLORATION
Think back to any time when you have wanted to say no, or have said no to a relationship. What body talk signals do you think you gave your potential partner?
● What postural signals; movement; body tension; breathing signs; facial expressions; eye signals, mouth signals, voice signals?

IMITATION: THE SINCEREST FLATTERY

What we like, we copy. If we fall in love, we copy on the deepest possible level. As our relationship develops, we begin to imitate our potential partner's way of behaving, by mirroring movements and matching his or her vocal tones and rhythms with our own.

Originally, we used the skill of imitation as children, to learn by example the basic elements of human behaviour: we copied the way our parents walked, talked, played and worked. As we grow, we mirror those people whom we admire, whose way of moving through the world seems to us worth having. If we are in love, then it is our partner whom we admire and with whom we will identify in this way.

So we may copy our partner's body posture, even down to matching exact gestures and minute head movements. Our voices may start to sound similar: we may find ourselves copying voice tone, accent or volume, dropping our voice at the same time, rising to a crescendo with our partner when excited or aroused. And if our lover reaches out to touch for emphasis, we will often meet the gesture half-way, reaching out in synchrony for mutual acknowledgement.

We also start to copy more subtle aspects of our partner's behaviour, of which we are un-aware: the depth of a smile, the crinkle of lines around the eyes, muscle tension or spinal twist. We will beat out together the exact rhythm of conversation, though often we will 'cross-match', using a complementary rather than identical way of moving; if our partner uses hands to empha-size something, for example, we may use our feet, or nod our head instead.

Yet the real wonder is that we can match, totally unconsciously, processes over which we would normally have no control. Lovers often move into synchrony with heartbeat, breathing and sweat rate, take on the same body heat or blink at the same speed. More surprising still, we

Below. Shared laughter is an obvious way of matching and mirroring, a noticeable signal that we have a rapport or are in love. Here, too, their entire posture mirrors; hand positions are the same, and they both lean forward in exactly the same way.

can even adopt, all unknowing, the same blood pressure as our mate!

We can, if we wish, utilize this knowledge to move closer to a potential partner. For if we find ourselves already matching and mirroring, we can take the decision to emphasize further this behaviour in order to hasten the process of identification. Slowly, subtly, without mimicry and with respect, we can take up another person's position, breathe with the same fre-quency and depth, take up the rhythm of the words spoken to us and match it in our own way. And, by being willing to synchronize so closely, we will show a potential partner that we can truly be trusted; it is then, perhaps, that our partner will start to copy us too.

Left. There is much matching and mirroring taking place between this couple. His hands move to mirror her arm position; their heads take on an identical tilt; their smiles are of equal depth. And look closely at the angle of each spine: similar muscle tension holds them in matching positions. The distance between them is a red herring; this couple is very close indeed.

Above. Waving hands move through the air and their message is clear. The shape they create and the horizontal movement they are making are the same in each case. She takes the lead in talking, and her hands are higher and more mobile, but his echo hers exactly as he joins in the conversation. What they are saying may be different, but here their rapport is very close indeed.

GETTING CLOSE

Right. They both know that she does not need help to get down, but it is nevertheless an ideal excuse to move their relationship on by making physical contact. Their smiles, the way they reach for each other long before it is really necessary and their eye contact all show that this is an emotional, not a practical, helping hand.

We have noticed each other; we have exchanged eye contact; we have moved near enough to speak. What are the next moves in the dance of intimacy, the moves that allow us to bridge the gap?

The time is now right for us to reach out and make actual physical contact. On a practical level, this opens up a whole new set of possibilities; once we can touch each other, we can support and receive support, comfort and receive comfort, and give and gain all kinds of information that we cannot get otherwise about our body heat, muscle tension, patterns of movement and emotional state.

We are not talking here about intimate contact; that comes later (*see* pages 56–57). This first touch is a bridging of the distance, a socially acceptable way of cutting through the personal-space zone we all keep around ourselves. And because it must be socially acceptable, while clearly stating an intention to progress our relationship, this first touch must follow the rules. It must be a brief touch, in case it is unwelcome for any reason. It must be a respectful touch, on extremities only – hand, elbow, shoulder, back – nowhere in the least sexual or threatening. At most, an arm can be slipped round the waist for a brief instant. But certainly no more. To save face on both sides, this first touch also has to be excusable. So he will take her arm as they cross the road, she will pat his shoulder in the middle of an explanation, he will hand her the wine in a way that means she has to touch his hand, she will stumble in a way that means he has to catch her. In these situations, we have an excuse: to guide; to emphasize; to exchange; to support. So if the touch is not accepted and reciprocated, then neither of us loses face.

For reciprocation is the final rule. We dance a complex dance of 'now me . . . now you'. We offer a touch, wait a while and expect a parallel touch – or an excuse for a touch – in return. If it does not happen, if she does not pass the wine back or he does not pat her shoulder in an equivalent way, we doubt if our offer was welcome. If other signals are positive – smiles, matching body movements, enthusiasm of voice tone – we will try again, offering another excusable contact. If this time there is still no reply, it is wise for us to withdraw at this stage, convinced without a word having been spoken to each other, that our offer has been refused.

Some people, however, are natural non-touchers. They may want to pursue the relationship, but have a higher personal-distance

Above. Moving closer gives them further information through both touch and smell. Our apocrine glands (in eyelids, armpits, nipples and genitals) give off scents which, research suggests, contain human equivalents of the pheromones which stimulate desire in animals. Such smells may also stimulate arousing memories of past partners. All of this tends to happen largely unconsciously: we may accept or reject partners because of their smell without knowing why.

> **EXPLORATION**
> Think back to when you and a partner touched for the very first time – not a sensual touch, but the introductory one. How did you, together, establish enough trust for this to happen? Particularly, what told you that it was fine for him or her to be touched by you? What was the first move and who made it? What 'excuse' was made for it to happen?

threshold than we have, so feel invaded by our touch and unwilling to attempt one of their own. They may be wary of being too forward, particularly if, as a man, they are conscious of the threat that their approach may present to a woman. They may be unaware of their own non-verbal communication and ours and, as a result, simply do not realize that we are actively encouraging them.

But if they under-respond, we will take this as a 'no', whether or not it is meant that way. Similarly, if someone over-responds – touching too soon, too long, too overtly or in the wrong place – we will retreat, convinced that any further intimate relationship with the offender would contain the same blend of invasion and insensitivity. A first touch can set up or demolish the possibility of an entire relationship.

The effective way to introduce touch is with care. Take one slow, acceptable, minimal step forward. Wait. Check out the answering touch. Wait. Take another slow, acceptable, minimal step forward. And wait for the response. It is all a little like climbing a glacier. The result, however, is very different. For once we have touched, been touched, and realized that we are both happy with the process, then the ice is broken. We can move forward to the next stage of our intimate relationship with more knowledge, and with more trust.

MAKING THE MOVES

In the process of getting together, every move we make counts. It is a sobering thought that everything we do at this early stage makes the difference between success and failure. It is an even more sobering thought that everything our potential partner does also makes or breaks the situation. Together, we win or lose.

He laughs, and she relaxes; she relaxes, so he feels more confident; he feels more confident, so she begins to confide; she confides, and he holds her hand to comfort her. They move forward in tandem. Yet every few minutes something could go wrong. With every small interaction there could be a potential hazard. His initial laugh could – completely unintentionally – sound like mockery; she might tense as a result; sensing her tension, he may withdraw, and soon she will decide that she has to go home early.

We normally manage to forestall such disasters. When we can sense them before they happen, we move to rectify the damage as each one looms. For example, if she does feel threatened when he laughs, and he notices, he will hasten to reassure her, openly or without words. This time the situation is saved, and they can move forward again.

But it may not always be as simple as that, for most of the elements that make the difference are ones both out of our awareness and our control. They are unconscious physiological reactions, subtle body-talk messages that neither we nor our potential partner can notice.

She can control where she looks but she has no influence whatsoever over her pupil dilation, which is what will show him whether she is really interested. He can wear the right after-shave but has no way of controlling his hormonal smell, which will tell her whether to go on or to back off. Both of them can control their overt gestures but will not be aware of the subliminal movements they make that signal 'I'm feeling nervous;

The photographs follow a male-female interaction from its beginnings through to intimate contact, telescoped into five typical moments.

Right. The diagram shows how the dynamic of an interaction can spiral upwards if both partners are making the right moves. They may move from eye contact (1) through to preening and displaying (2). Encouraged by this the couple may move close enough to talk (3) and later confide an emotion, thus indicating intimacy (4). Laughter (5) deepens their rapport. One or the other creates an excuse to touch (6). By this time they will be matching each other on many levels (7).

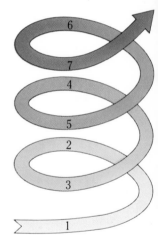

he looks too sure of himself; she seems trustworthy; he has a nice sense of humour'.

What is the answer? If you see a potential partner's gaze slipping away, or if you hear his or her voice becoming flat and uninterested and you have no idea what has caused it, then act. Do something different: anything will do. Move closer, further away, breathe slower or faster, laugh or cry. If what has gone wrong is out of your consciousness, then you cannot consciously put it right. So have the courage to try something different and to keep going until something eventually works.

Below. They begin apart, uneasy with each other. He displays in a classic male way, talking animatedly; she listens with downcast eyes and we sense that, at this point, he may not be making too good an impression. Things soon develop, however. He has perhaps sensed her unease and, coming forward, has invited her to talk. Something, conscious or unconscious, changes her mind. She now feels safe to talk, and is perhaps confiding in him. They are soon sharing a joke, laughing together and relaxed; though guarded, their positions are increasingly matched and they now have eye contact.

Left. The eye contact has worked its magic, as has shared laughter. Their faces are lifted towards each other and he has reached out a hand to take hers. She is still a little wary, her arm across her body, but they are talking more equally now, taking turns and finding common ground. Perhaps now they are closer, and reading signals of smell and touch, they are each finding subconscious reasons why getting friendly is a good idea.

Right. They are far into the intimate distance zone, and could well kiss soon, communicating with all five senses. And all senses, conscious and unconscious, signal success here. They see that their body posture, head angle and depth of smile are matching quite remarkably. They will be hearing reassuring tones and rhythms in each other's voice. As they are staying so close, taste, smell and touch must be right. Their interaction is undoubtedly working.

Chapter Two
MOVING TO INTIMACY

As we begin to realize that we do indeed have a relationship with another person, then we also have to begin to move towards greater intimacy, on both emotional and physical levels. We need to open up, to allow the other person to know increasingly what we think and feel. And this is the time to let our partner see more and more of our body, our sensuality, our sexuality. The challenge of such exposure is real, but infinitely worthwhile.

This is the stage of learning about each other, of building the foundations for the rich sexual life we hope to have. By using body talk to become aware of our own desires and to read our partner's likes and dislikes, we begin to chart the elements that make both of us who we are, in bed and out of it. We can start genuinely to please each other, knowing that sexual fulfilment will be one of the doorways to a rewarding relationship.

We need to look at a wide range of elements, however, if we are truly to understand ourselves and our partner. We need to examine the context of our past to understand what has made us who we are. We need to master the art of intimate communication, to understand what we are really saying when we touch, kiss or explore each other's bodies. And we need to understand the reasons why we sometimes hold back from disclosure, refusing to reveal ourselves further, either physically or emotionally. But, by using body talk to guide us through the maze, we can emerge together from this period of exploration, intimately connected and ready to make love work.

Getting close can create very different feelings. Here, she is cuddling up, allowing her sheer enjoyment to come through in her externally focussed smile and the relaxed touch of her hand against his chest. His vulnerable expression shows us that for him the experience is altogether a more serious one; he is internally focussed as he comes to terms with what he feels, and his hand pulling her towards him shows his need and desire.

STEPS TO INTIMACY

When we move towards intimacy, we move in carefully defined stages. Too slowly or too fast, and we find ourselves stranded and out of touch with our partner whose unwritten rules we are breaking.

We first meet, we first talk, we first flirt. We move in closer to personal distance, and then closer still to intimate distance. We touch, hug and kiss each other. After this, intimacy follows steadily: taking clothes off, touching upper and then lower body, masturbation, sexual intercourse and oral sex.

But we have very different ideas about how to time steps to intimacy. Western culture, for example, moves steadily through the stages, while Eastern or very religious cultures wait until after commitment before moving through all the sexual stages together, often in one night. There are also individual differences. Some see oral sex as a stage to intimacy before the commitment of intercourse; while others would place oral sex at the end of the risk line, only to be tried once everything else has been achieved. Men traditionally wish to move quickly, while women move more slowly although this balance is changing. Our situation, too, may dictate the pace. Holidays, conferences or any context where we are in close contact make the acceptable speed much quicker than it otherwise would be.

The way we handle these stages can both make and mar a relationship; if we and a partner are in agreement as to which stage comes where, and how fast we should move, then all will be smooth. If not, we may judge the other person harshly and not always consistently. A man who holds back may be seen as unmasculine; if he moves more quickly than she does, he will be seen as pressurizing or uninvolved. A woman who moves forward quickly can be viewed as

Left. Older couples, perhaps with past unhappiness behind them, may need to take a slow path to intimacy. They will develop their friendship and mutual respect for a long time before moving on to sexual involvement. Alternatively, knowing the joys of sexuality, they may have fewer barriers to early love-making than younger people have.

Left. First love is a vital stage. Losing virginity, in any culture, is also a step not to be taken lightly. There is more social pressure for women to keep their virginity than there is for men, so she may need to be more convinced of the importance and durability of the relationship than he will before saying yes.

Left. A closed-mouth kiss is sometimes a first move towards intimacy in a new relationship. It may mean that a partner wants to go no further in intimacy for the moment, and it is a myth that a closed-mouth response will always succumb to a continuing firm kiss. More likely, this will create an irreversible resistance!

Left. An open-mouth kiss is often used by him to test whether love-making would be both acceptable and enjoyable. For her, on the other hand, it may be simply a stage along the route, a long way from a commitment to full love-making.

cheap; if slowly as a prude or frigid, while a rapid move through the early stages followed by a slower pace may be seen as teasing.

How can we tell if our steps to intimacy are mismatched? If physical arousal is just not there, then it is likely we are moving too fast; if emotional or physical frustration is constant, we will think we are moving too slowly. And if there is irritation, battles of the 'You would if you loved me ... You wouldn't ask if you cared ...' variety, then something needs to be done.

Usually, the hesitant partner is not emotionally able to move more quickly unless the whole partnership is at stake. It is the partner who is moving more quickly who may feel able to slow down. In fact, this can be a benefit. In a loving relationship when time is on your side, moving slowly can be a delightful way to learn about each other, physically as well as emotionally, before moving on.

EXPLORATION

Rearrange these steps to intimacy in the order that would feel totally right to you. Then work out how much time would have to pass in between each stage – minutes, hours, days, weeks, months, years – for you to feel good about yourself, your partner and the relationship. What could you or a partner do to speed up or to slow down the process?

● Visual contact; oral sex; first eye contact; move to personal distance; touching of lower body; first touch; move to intimate distance; intercourse; first body hug; first touch of hand to face; touching of upper body; taking clothes off; first conversation; mutual masturbation; first kiss.

YOUR SEXUAL HISTORY

Our present sexuality is inextricably linked to our past memories. Our childhood forms our identity as sexual adults, is woven into our way of looking at the world and glimpsed in every aspect of our body talk.

How does this happen? As our body matures, our direct experience of the world around us creates our developing sexuality. So, for example, a glimpse of satin underwear, the overheard sounds of our parents making love, a sex-education lesson at school and a forbidden video will all combine to create not only our desires but also our sexual potential. What we like and dislike in bed, what we are afraid of and what we are compulsed towards in sex all have their roots in such previous, formative experiences.

The influence of the past does not end with childhood, however. Bragging in the pub, giggling in the kitchen, we learn from friends what it is like to have sex. We lose our virginity, and the ecstasy or trauma of that event remains with us for the rest of our life. A caring partner teaches us sexual inventiveness, and a rejecting one teaches us inhibition and disgust. When we begin a new relationship, we bring to it a Pandora's box of distress and delight, as does our new partner.

So how is it possible for us to tell when the past is influencing the present? The fact is that it always does, but it will be most apparent when body talk brings it to our notice. Our emotions, or those of our partner can, without warning, link into something that is not in the here and now. A reminiscent smile as we remember a wonderful past orgasm, a new position suddenly recalled from an old relationship, a shiver as we are touched again in the same way as when we first experienced real passion: all these are examples of body talk telling us that we are no longer rooted firmly in the present, and that some part of us has started to reminisce.

The memories may not always be positive. A sudden, inexplicable tensing-up that is nothing to do with our partner, a memory that cuts across passion and reduces us to tears, an unwillingness to do or be done to that interrupts normally delightful love-making: all these are past traumas resurfacing as present distress.

If the emotion is very strong, it may drag us all the way back to childlike behaviour whenever it is experienced. Partners who sound or act much younger than they are, who curl up in our arms or rock back and forth are almost certainly in the grip of a very early memory. And partners who use 'teacher words' – 'I shouldn't be doing this really... we mustn't go any further...', as if they are recalling past messages from strict adults – are almost certainly being strongly influenced by their past.

Awareness of sexual history can mean the difference between reading body talk as if it were an infant primer, or as if it were a work of literature. For if we can realize that our body talk is rooted in the past, it will immediately become more understandable and acceptable. If we can respond to our partner's tension when touched by realizing that it is the memory of past sexual invasion that is distressing, then the issue will be half solved. By explaining to our partner that our fear about love-making is based on our experiences in a past unhappy relationship rather than his or her presence, then we will be turning a problem into an opportunity for both emotional and physical intimacy.

Equally, allowing ourselves to reach back into our past for delightfully erotic memories and use them to enhance our present sexuality will let us draw on a treasure chest of possibilities. And realizing that, here and now, loving touch is setting up all kinds of good experiences for the future will create a sexual resource that will last throughout our life.

Source	Female	Male
Early childhood messages	Seeing Mum and Dad that time.	I'll show mine if you show yours.
Religious or cultural beliefs	Nice girls don't.	Does it matter if I'm circumcised?
Sex education at school	That silly biology lesson.	Learning the truth about AIDS.
Peer-group pressure	I was the last to buy a bra.	That time in the showers after games.
Losing virginity	Why didn't the earth move for me?	It took such a long time.
Sexual partners	Rob ... mmm!	Lucy taught me such a lot.
Negative experiences	Having a positive smear.	Not being able to get it up that time.

Below. Our early experience of our parents' ease or unease with nudity and sexuality will form our own attitudes. If we learn as a child that bodies are pleasurable, we take that knowledge with us into adulthood.

Above. Some typical messages we can receive about our sexuality. They come from different sources and may change our attitudes and feelings as we grow. Write down some messages you have received about sexuality.

READING THE MESSAGES

If you really want to excel in body talk, then forget the rules. Ignore the guidelines. Throw out all the expert body of knowledge about non-verbal communication and create your own. Rules and guidelines are vital to give us generalized expertise about what body talk does and how it works. But if you are in an intimate relationship, then this is something very specific. Your partner is a unique individual and so are you. Your relationship is a unique one. And so you need to learn to chart specifically what happens for you and your partner.

First, you need to learn to read your partner's body talk in a very precise way. Notice the way in which he or she walks, talks, smiles when excited, looks when confused, and how his or her voice tone changes when querying something. You need to learn tiny, minimal signals, such as those listed in the exploration box on the opposite page; many of these elements are also described in more detail elsewhere in this book.

This may sound difficult, but you have a head start: you are involved with your partner. And, particularly at the start of a relationship, you will be watching your partner constantly, listening with delight, smelling, tasting and touching compulsively. Love is the best teacher of all.

Once you have begun to notice the tiny signals your partner gives, then start to make distinctions. What is the difference between your partner's smile when excited and when nervous? There will be differences: perhaps a raised eyebrow; a skin colour change or a twist of the mouth. How does your partner's voice differ when querying something from when sure of something: a higher tone; a rise in rhythm at the end of a sentence; a brief pause midway through? How does your partner's touch alter if he or she suddenly becomes nervous: instant sweating; a change in body temperature; a tension beneath the surface of the skin? Learn to

Above. To read the signs correctly we must set aside expectations and consider only what we actually see. She is in an office environment, but we must not assume that she is thinking about work. We will only know this by comparing her typical postures and expressions while thinking about work with what she is displaying now. In fact, her defocussed eyes, the tilted angle of her head and her slight smile all suggest thoughts more centred around her lover than her job.

calibrate, getting a consistent check on the differences between one smile and another, between one voice tone and another, between one touch and another.

The benefits are endless. Of course you want to understand your partner better in a general sense; but learning to calibrate his or her range of body-talk signals gives you an ability accurately to gauge mood, needs and wants that will take your relationship deeper than ever before. You will be able to tell how a partner is feeling before you are told, and sense subtle reactions even from an unsure lover.

Above. She assumes a similar position, but this time in a home setting. Here, she is more likely to be thinking of personal matters, but again we need to be careful not to jump to any conclusions. Her distant gaze may be assessing her love potential, but equally may be assessing the current sales figure for a work project. Her angled head position could mean she is thinking of her lover's voice, or considering which decision to make about clothes, car or garden.

EXPLORATION

Ask your partner to think of something sensual (or even sexual) that he or she enjoys doing, and then something non-sensual that is disliked. Check the way your partner's signals change while doing this. If you can, notice any sounds too; hold hands and check if there is any change in what you feel. Use the check-list *below* to notice further differences in response when thinking of the two, very different, things.

● Things to look for:
Body position
Body movements and gestures
Internal or external focus
Facial expression
Mouth signals (opening, reddening of lips, change of shape of mouth)
Eye signals (direction, shape, pupil dilation, moisture)
Depth and breathing movement
Skin colour change
● Things to listen for:
Breathing
Heart rate
Tiny sounds
● Things you can feel:
Skin tone
Moisture
Warmth

Essentially, you are learning the art of prediction. If you can learn that a particular glance means he is feeling angry, then you can prepare for – or forestall – the row. If you know that her cheeks flush when she is feeling sexy, then you can move in at the right moment.

You need to be careful. Sometimes the signals you receive are not the ones that are being sent. If you are feeling any strong emotion – be that lust or love as well as irritation or wariness – this may block you from interpreting correctly. And your partner may be sending out mixed messages, feeling a whole range of emotions, so that you become confused and cannot clearly understand what is happening. Take your time, particularly if your relationship is new. Loving understanding is worth waiting for.

All these skills are ones you are developing anyway, just by being close to someone; you learn to know a partner, and what he or she is going to say next, just by being together. It is often called intuition, the careful and loving tuning in to your partner's signals and the ability to use them wisely. But body talk helps you understand intuition, learn its skills and put them to the best use, in and out of bed.

SENDING THE SIGNALS

One half of body talk is about calibrating the unspoken communication of our partner; the other is about listening to ourselves. For to become body-talk experts, we have to listen to our own feelings, as our arousal ebbs and flows and as we move towards or away from pleasure. We must use the same calibration skills for our own internal processes as we use to chart our partner's external signs. Then, once aware, we must communicate these signals to others, making our body talk clear and easy to read.

Our body has a range of inner signs. The sensations on our skin urge us to move closer to our partner's warm body; the sensitive nerves on the lips respond under the pressure of a kiss. Our heartbeat rises, our breath becomes shorter, we begin to feel undeniable pleasure all over our body, a pleasure which says 'do this more'.

Alternatively, if all is not right, our body gives out very different signs: a clammy sweat when touch is invasive, tension around our mouth at a clumsy kiss. These negative signals are vital in raising our sexual potential because they teach us what to avoid as well as seek; so the more aware we are, the more our pleasure increases.

Many signals, such as blood pressure or body smell, will be outside our awareness. In one particular case, however, we can learn to do consciously what all humans do unconsciously, that is to check out what we are feeling in our 'comfort zone'. This particular area of our body, usually our stomach or back, signals to us whether what we are experiencing is right for us. When everything is fine, there is a feeling of relaxation and stillness; when something is wrong, there is tension or uneasy movement. Our comfort zone gives us the go-ahead (or the stop sign) in many areas of our life: small issues such as whether to take an umbrella today, large issues such as whether to take a job. In sexuality too, we can learn to become aware of what our comfort zone is telling us, whether this is the right place, time, person and move.

The next step is to learn to signal our intuitions to our partner; moves towards, moves away, shifts and alterations help us find together the best things to do. And, with partners to whom we are especially close, we can develop these natural accommodations even further. We can work out a specific, consistent, personalized code that allows us to communicate precisely what is happening. Perhaps this code may be based on sound: a hum, higher and higher, to let our partner know that what is happening to us is increasingly good; a complex system of indrawn breaths that shows when the sensation is just right. Perhaps the code is based on touch: a fingertip signal to mean pull back or come closer; a particular use of the tongue to say 'I'm ready to take clothes off now'.

As we develop our relationship, so our sexual code develops. In the long-term, our communication of needs and desires can be immediate, precise and devastatingly effective.

EXPLORATION

Take time alone to explore your own internal body talk. Once you are comfortable and relaxed, think of some pleasant sexual memory, maybe a particularly good love-making experience or a fantasy that you enjoy. Notice how your body responds. Where in your body do you feel most sensation? How would you describe the sensations: hot/cold; moving/still; fast/slow; hard/soft; heavy/light ... any other words you can think of? Concentrate particularly on how your skin feels. What sensations do you experience at different points on your skin? How would you describe them? Be aware of any differences in your body reactions: does your breathing change; can you hear your heart beating faster; do you sweat more? How could you communicate how you feel to your partner in an effective way that could enhance your love-making?

She takes the time to find out more about what her body likes and responds to. By touching, exploring, pausing and continuing, she discovers precisely what she feels when she is aroused.

SETTING THE SCENE

Whether we are making the first move or making love for the thousandth time, we need to set the scene. What are the surroundings saying about us and about our relationship that will create a positive experience?

First, consider territory. Does it matter whether we are in the safety of our own home, or the comparative strangeness of our partner's? Do we need to be in a neutral place, such as a hotel or a friend's flat? Do we need to be comfortably indoors, or in the wildness of a wood or a beach? At the start of a relationship, emotional safety is usually uppermost for both partners; as we gradually build trust, then we can afford to experiment further afield.

Think next about what to remove from the setting. Chairs with arms and coffee tables between seats are inhibiting barriers, although too few barriers can, by reducing distance too soon or by reminding us of sexual potential too early, create a sense of danger, forcing both partners into erecting emotional barriers.

Distractions too need to go. Take the phone off the hook or switch on the answering machine, and arrange a time with flat-mates before which they will stay away. Pets can distract, though an

Right. She has created a setting of utter sensuality with warm, rich colours blending with each other, and with the clothes both people are wearing. The room contains a wealth of textures, from the sofa brocade to the smooth wood of the table and the softness of the flowers and ferns. There are few barriers – the sofa gives clear space between them – and there are no distractions in sight. The sunlight comes dimly through what we guess are drawn blinds, and the whole atmosphere is one of unthreatening sensuality. And yet, perhaps there are also some less positive signs in this room. The sofa itself allows them to sit separately, a long way apart. Its contours suggest a firmness, perhaps hardness incompatible with later love-making. Their glasses are separate with no jug or bottle to give an excuse for hands to touch as they pour a second helping. And the light shining in his eyes makes him unable clearly to read her expression or to make eye contact with her. It is unclear what will happen next. Her arm reaches out to him but there is still distance between them.

EXPLORATION
When setting the scene for love, be sure to check these elements:
- Your place or your partner's?
- What should you leave and what should be removed?
- Any distractions that should go?
- Things to stimulate the senses: sight; sound; smell; taste; touch.

affectionate cat or small dog can provide a sensual focus for early contact.

Include in the setting elements that run the whole spectrum of the senses. Is the room visually appealing, with colours that match and complement each other? Is the lighting subtle, able to be dimmed as passions rise? Are there appealing sounds to heighten the mood? (Music is the traditional scene-setter, but wind chimes can work just as well.) Make sure that there are things to touch and to be touched, a range of tactile experiences from stone to velvet, from lace to gleaming wood, that will raise sensual

awareness and so heighten desire. Complete the spectrum by stimulating the senses of taste and smell: pot pourri, fresh flowers, food, wine. Warmth allows the removal of clothes when the time is right.

Keep the setting subtle. Any of the elements mentioned above can act as a turn-off if overdone. Too much music, too much wine, an unmade bed, any overt signs of impending sexuality spell danger to either gender, particularly at the start of a relationship. The real importance of setting the scene is not to steamroller into seduction, but to make it easy for two people to contact their desire for each other. And in that sense, the most vital aspect of any setting is the way in which it reflects those who are in it. The biggest turn-on will be a room that says who we are, even if that room happens to be cool, well-lit, and utterly free of sounds, smells and tastes.

As we learn about each other and what we like, we can therefore begin to customize. If smooth textures increase desire, choose satin sheets or drape parachute silk round the bed. If a particular scent makes pulses race, keep some under the pillow. Emphasize the importance of the relationship by displaying photographs of your partner; emphasize the importance of novelty by displaying erotic pictures. Sexual music need not be heavy and rhythmic, it may simply be a favourite song. Sexual taste may not be caviar and champagne: for some of us, cornflakes and orange juice in bed, between orgasms, can be just as satisfying.

A final thought. If our intention is to say no to sex tonight, we can signal this by contradicting the above guidelines: set up furniture barriers, introduce distractions, turn lights up full and play music that makes for thinking rather than feeling. But be warned; these signs may signal no forever rather than no just for tonight.

TALKING IT THROUGH

Sometimes, however good our non-verbal communication, we have to talk. Whether it is our need for touch or our need for commitment, perhaps our delight about the future or our regret about the past, we need to put things into words and have those words accepted and respected by our partner.

But talking is often the hardest thing to do. We may be afraid because our experiences in past relationships have taught us that it is not all right to talk about sex, that lovers react badly to any hint of need or want, or that we will be rejected if we dare to voice our feelings. Our body talk will tell us when we are indeed wary of talking things through, or when our partner is similarly wary. Through body talk we can also ease the way to letting out the words.

If we are on the point of confiding but find ourselves sitting silently with fingers to mouth then something is wrong. If our partner is displaying certain signals – chewing the lips, clenching the teeth subtly or biting the fingers – then speech is evidently a problem at this time. If we notice the tiniest of movements around the mouth, then we can be sure that there are words that are trying to get spoken and failing in the attempt. Amazing as it may seem, these body signals show us, quite literally, holding back the words. We want to speak out, but our fear makes us move to hide our mouth, bite our lips, stop the words from being heard. Another signal to look out for is when a partner's eyes gaze directly to the left or right without focussing, as if looking hopelessly for inspiration.

She needs to talk, but she cannot face eye contact. He sits as close as he can, turned towards her, touching her with one side of his body and angling his head. He is looking at her so that, when she is ready, she can turn to meet his gaze.

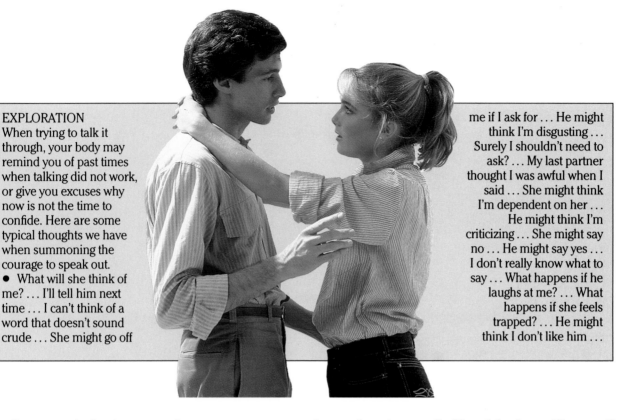

When trying to talk it through, your body may remind you of past times when talking did not work, or give you excuses why now is not the time to confide. Here are some typical thoughts we have when summoning the courage to speak out.
● What will she think of me? ... I'll tell him next time ... I can't think of a word that doesn't sound crude ... She might go off me if I ask for ... He might think I'm disgusting ... Surely I shouldn't need to ask? ... My last partner thought I was awful when I said ... She might think I'm dependent on her ... He might think I'm criticizing ... She might say no ... He might say yes ... I don't really know what to say ... What happens if he laughs at me? ... What happens if she feels trapped? ... He might think I don't like him ...

Once we do begin to speak, we may not say exactly what we mean; again, non-verbal communication can betray us. To discover if you or your partner is holding back, stop listening to the words; listen instead to the way words are spoken. Stutters and stumbles; repeated or mistaken words; sentences switched or incomplete; incoherent sounds: all these show that what we are saying is not what we really want to say. Underneath, the real story is desperately trying to get out.

The way to break the silence is to stop trying to get the words out. Whether it is you blocking your confidences, or your partner who is struggling to speak, opt for body talk instead. Cut through the fear by seeking or offering the best reassurance in the world: supportive touch. Hold a hand, give a hug; and in particular, touch the comfort zone, which almost certainly will be tense and anxious. If it is not the right moment to talk just then, you will know it, either because your own signals warn you against it or because your partner shows signs of anxiety again when he or she tries to talk. The right time will come if you have the patience to wait.

If this really is the time for talking, then accompany it by physical support. Try face-to-face eye contact or, if that makes you uneasy, as much body contact as you can handle, sitting side by side or cuddled up. Try holding your partner from behind if a comfort zone is on the back, or laying a hand on the stomach if that is where anxiety is felt. These are effective body-talk ways of reassuring your partner, of saying 'I'm here, I'm supporting you, I'm listening'.

When words do start to flow, let them come. If you are the one talking, keep going until you feel more relaxed. If your partner is confiding, you can help by signalling understanding and empathy with a smile, a firmer hug, eye contact or a nod. Only begin to respond with words when you are sure your partner is ready, for words are often a subtle attempt to shut other people up and may be perceived by your partner as such. If you really want to let the words through, then keep listening and keep holding.

SENSUAL SIGNALS

How do we sense first arousal? The inspired lover can tell just what level of desire a partner has reached, and knows when it rises and when it falls.

Our own body gives us signals we cannot ignore: a feeling of warmth, for example, tingling all over, a shiver down the spine or a rush of feeling to mouth or fingertips. Our comfort zone may tremble or quiver in anticipation. She is likely to feel varied sensations, on her nipples, the muscles of her back, her thighs, the palms of her hands or her stomach. He will feel more focussed sensation, increased sensitivity around his mouth, and the stirrings of an erection.

Movement as we become aroused will vary; perhaps we will hardly move as passion comes upon us, perhaps we will feel the urge to act and respond. Our partner's movements will change, touching us – with body, mouth, hands and tongue – in a harder and more demanding way. This touch gradually speeds up and takes on a rhythm of its own as our partner moves closer and presses against us. And, as we become mutually aroused, we will increasingly match each other in body movements and rhythms.

We will also focus more and more internally; lost in our own sensations, we move from consciously noticing what our partner is doing and experience instead his or her movements as increasingly part of our own.

There are also many body-talk signals that are not under conscious control. We cannot, by thinking, alter our sweat rate, bring on an erection or increase the sensitivity of our skin. Because these signs are outside our control, they are undeniable ways of signalling arousal ourselves and of checking our partner's desire.

So, as we continue to build our relationship, we will know what is giving pleasure and what is not, by constantly calibrating the progress of our own and our partner's sensual signals.

Below. As she becomes aroused, her eyes mist over, losing focus or closing with trembling lids. Her skin becomes firmer and warmer, her face and body covered with a film of sweat that may change in taste or smell as desire rises.

Below. Long eye contact, often with pupil dilation, is a typical sign of sensuality. Her mouth may open, her tongue appearing in readiness to kiss. Her lips get fuller and more sensitive, her mouth very dry or moist.

Left. As she starts to become even more aroused, blood rushes to her skin, bringing a flush to her face, neck and chest. Later, as desire increases, this flush may deepen and spread across her breasts and stomach. This parallels the rush of blood to all other parts of her body, preparing them for the physical stimulation and demands brought by love-making.

Below. All attention moves internally to focus on the skin. The muscle tone will change, leaving it relaxed and supple, or increasingly firm. There may be a trembling, or a quivering of nerves under the surface; the skin becomes far more sensitive, although we can nevertheless override any discomfort or even pain we may feel in the pleasure of arousal.

Left. Voice tone changes as arousal rises; there may be fewer words but the tone will drop, become more husky, softer, deeper, slower and perhaps more trembling. Hear too the heart rate and breathing rate rise as adrenalin pumps into the body; breath may come in deep gulps or fast, shallow ones to supply oxygen; blood pressure may rise too. All these biological responses prepare the body for action.

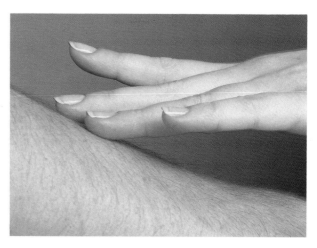

LEADER OR FOLLOWER

In every partnership, there is always a balance of leading and following. Traditionally, he always took charge, initiating sex, changing position, leading her through the process. She responded; any initiative was seen, even recently, as meaning that she was maybe a little too experienced for her own good.

Things are very different now. We value leadership from both sexes and recognize that, even if neither is actively taking charge, one of us may well be subtly leading from behind, making things happen with unconscious signals of touch or breathing, creating the rhythm with unnoticeable changes of speed or pressure. We also recognize that, in any love-making session, we can take it in turns to lead, alternating suggestions and compliance, sometimes moving and sometimes loving to be moved.

Be aware of the ways in which you and your partner lead and follow during love-making: the leader may move the other partner into a position that feels right, or move back and encourage the other to follow; it is also the leader who will shift, ease over, speed up, hold back. The follower will be happier to go with the movements, not making overt suggestions, but reacting with delight to what is being offered; muscles and limbs will be soft and responsive, and happy to move and then stop with a partner's guidance.

Often confused with leading and following is doing and being done to. Some of us never use these 'roles' in love-making; they are preferences in style rather than control mechanisms, and we will often alternate between them. When we are the doer we like to act, kissing or masturbating, giving oral sex or thrusting; we are externally focussed, noticing and checking response; and we delight in watching a partner respond: the joy of responding is, for us, a lesser one.

Conversely, we may like to be done to,

revelling in receiving pleasure, and knowing that we are actually giving it by allowing our partner the active role. Internally focussed, we tend to shut our eyes, go still or lose ourselves completely in our sensations. We love feeling our partner act upon us; the thrill of acting and arousing is not for us – at least not this time.

If we tend to take the same approach consistently – leader, follower, doer or receiver – we may find a partner who totally fits with us, providing complementary skills. We can move together to provide love-making that meets the needs of both of us, and does not demand that we take up roles with which we are not, essentially, relaxed and content.

If we are with a partner who does not complement us, however, there can be problems: if two leaders make love, they often clash horns, while two followers may spiral love-making down into an action-less event. Two doers will vie for the pleasure of acting upon each other; two receivers will get confused because neither partner is doing the giving. Equally, if we expect a partner who is primarily a receiver to give pleasure, we may label him or her selfish. If we expect a lover to receive who only knows how to give, we may think him or her too controlling. Each pattern needs a balance, with two people working together to make a complete whole.

The secret is to have the motivation and the ability to switch roles, and to be emotionally flexible. So if we read our partner's body talk and realize we are dealing with a leader, we may want to take the follower role for a while; if we know that our partner is a receiver, our best route is to act sometimes as a doer and enjoy our partner's pleasure. In time, as our needs match, we will both be able to assume any of these four roles in bed and then, with a perfect balance, create a perfect harmony.

Left. What is actually happening here? It seems as if he is about to chase her, but it is she who is egging him on. She wants to be done to, but she is taking the lead in encouraging him to do. He is turning, smiling and happy to follow, but responding to her initiation rather than taking charge himself. The body talk displayed here shows that reference to 'dominance', 'submission' and 'initiating' in sex is misleading. In all co-operative and enjoyable sexual encounters, even when we seem at our most passive, we are subtly indicating what we want by movement, by expression, by a slight intake of breath. Only in truly non-co-operative sex, where someone is, without enjoyment, giving in to another's demands, could it really be said that only one partner is in control.

EXPLORATION

Look at the statements that follow. In each case, tick the one that most applies to you. Next, consult the key to find out what each answer reveals about you.

1(a) I prefer to act on my lover.
 (b) I prefer my lover to act on me.
2(a) I like to go with what is happening in bed.
 (b) I like to think ahead, planning the next position.
3(a) In sex, I like to be the doer.
 (b) In sex, I like to be done to.
4(a) I initiate sex less often than my lover.
 (b) I initiate sex more often than my lover.

5(a) In sex, I love the feeling of my lover signalling what he or she wants.
 (b) In sex, I love the feeling of signalling what I want.
6(a) If we are fighting, I like to lose.
 (b) If we are fighting, I like to win.
7(a) I tend to set the pace in sex.
 (b) I am happy to let my lover set the pace.

Key
Leader: 2(b); 4(b); 5(b); 7(a)
Follower: 2(a); 4(a); 5(a); 7(b)
Doer: 3(a); 1(a); 6(b)
Receiver: 3(b); 1(b); 6(a)

TOUCH TALK

When we touch and are touched, we give a message far more immediate than any words or looks could express.

Touch is the first way we ever communicate. In the early weeks of life, when our eyes do not yet focus and our mind makes no sense of words, touch is our main channel of communication with the world. As we mature, touch reminds us of these early times when we were safe and loved, and becomes an unfailing way of transmitting affection and support. When we grow to learn passion as adults, touch becomes its main channel of expression, allowing us to retreat from sight and sound and simply experience the world through our skin.

What variations in touch allow us to communicate and to calibrate? The part of the body we choose to touch is the first indicator of what we are communicating; quite simply, the more intimate the part, the more intimate the touch. A whole body hug is very different from a mouth-to-ear kiss. Reaching out a hand is a move towards intimacy or comradeship, while touching feet is more likely to be a signal between established lovers. Rubbing noses, a formal greeting signal for Polynesians, would be a fun sign of intimacy in the West; while 'butterfly kissing' with eyelashes is a gentle sign of lovers' affection for each other.

Next, look at how we touch. Do we stroke? Do we rub? Do we tickle, scratch, massage, pinch, pummel or smack? All can be incredibly erotic; all can equally well signal a change of mood to playfulness, urgent need or even anger. Only the context tells which.

Each aspect of touch – pressure, speed and rhythm – can be seen to carry a subtly different message. A light, soft touch with little pressure may signal erotic teasing. The touch may become firmer and heavier as passion increases. But be wary: lightness may mean that the toucher is

Above. Her hand gently but firmly tilts his face towards her while her lips brush lightly against his ear. Her other hand supports him, flat and firm against his back, while her whole body moves against him, providing warmth and closeness.

Right. She moves closer while he, in response, holds on to her more firmly. Her breath is warm on his ear, and we can see his arousal as his head turns and his mouth begins to open.

unsure; while firmness may indicate a non-sexual trust and closeness. Slow speed and regular rhythm will signal relaxation or reassurance, the speed rising with the desire, the rhythm alternating to create erotic interest.

Warmth and moisture are undeniable clues: skin will warm and dampen with emotion or passion, while a cold touch, be it dry or clammy, will usually signal anxiety or uncertainty.

The key to all touch talk is matching response to need. If you know that your partner's need is for comfort and security, try a whole body hug, firm and steady, with maybe a little rocking movement for reassurance. Once desire begins to rise, try starting with light, soft, slow touches, moving gradually into stronger, more rhythmical movements. But people have individual wants; light, fast, teasing movements may be perfect for her, while he may want firm, regular stroking from the very first touch.

Above. She bites and licks his ear while stroking his neck. The touch of tongue in ear is reflective: what is happening reflects what could happen elsewhere on the body. Here, her tongue in his ear mirrors her tongue in his mouth or his penis in her vagina. Reflective touch at the start of a relationship can both indicate that we are ready for more intimate steps, and also check out whether our partner is happy for us to go further. For established partners, it is a happy reminder of what is to come.

MOUTH MUSIC

With our mouth, as babies, we took nourishment from the world. Later, we tested out everything we saw by biting, gnawing or chewing. If it tasted good, we liked it.

In the same way, as we become more intimate with a partner, we offer them our mouth. A sign of wanting to be close, it is also our way to test out whether closeness is the right step. Does this person taste right? Do we taste right to them?

Mouths are made for communication. When we are aroused, our lips engorge with blood, increasing their sensitivity. Sebaceous glands at the edge of our lips and in our mouth produce semio-chemicals that also signal arousal.

Equally, mouths are made for us to create responses in our partner. We can perform an amazing permutation of movements as we blow, suck, breathe, lick, bite and kiss. Lovers aware of body-talk possibilities will move from one to the other easily, varying the pressure, speed and rhythm and matching the movement to the mood. The particular warmth and moisture of mouths, and the possibilities created by softness or hardness of lips, tongue, and the firm biting edge of teeth can bring forth very particular responses on many parts of the body.

Mouths also communicate by their response. If a partner's mouth opens and allows us in, then we are gaining a positive reaction. If a partner's tongue comes to meet ours, then desire is rising. A firm, erect tongue is certainly aroused while a soft, yielding tongue may indicate a preferred style of slower love-making. Is there increased moisture, or does our partner prefer a dry kiss? We may even notice changes in smell and taste from the chemicals produced by the sebaceous glands, telling us when it is time to move on to the next stage of passion. By varying our own mouth music and then calibrating our partner's response, we will soon be able to find a style that matches the needs of both of us.

Above. A closed-mouth kiss between intimate partners is used for public greeting or for a pause in sensuality. Between potential partners, it often signifies one partner slowing things down.

Above. Mouths open and tongues intertwine in a kiss that reflects eventual love-making, giving them essential clues to their needs in later sexual intercourse.

EXPLORATION

What kind of kiss do you like at the start of love-making, as desire rises and as you progress to intercourse? Think of these elements:

- Open or closed mouth
- Hard or soft lips
- A regular or irregular rhythm
- Hard or soft pressure
- Slow or more urgent speed
- Tongue used a lot; a little; not at all
- Lips and tongue wet or dry
- Tongue soft or erect
- Speed and rhythm of tongue movement

Above. She uses her hands gently on his head to move the kiss in the direction she wishes. Leaning back into his hand, she begins to kiss his face while he takes her lower lip between his teeth.

Left. By pulling him to her, arms round his neck, she signals her need for a deeper kiss. Pressure, rhythm, speed and depth of both mouth and tongue will change with arousal, though whether that change is from slow to fast, from soft to hard or vice versa, will vary according to individual needs.

TO TOUCH OR NOT TO TOUCH

Our body is our territory. We guard it well, until the time comes for us to allow people we trust over the threshold. And so, at the start of any relationship, we may find that some areas are for touching and that others are not, at least not for the moment.

We progress slowly through our individual go and no-go areas. We allow friends and new lovers access to the periphery of our body and, as we gain trust, literally allow them closer and closer to the centre of our personal territory.

How we do this varies. Our upbringing may mean that some areas are not to be touched in a particular way, such as touching the genitals with the tongue. Age usually brings fewer no-go areas, though traumatic experiences such as sexual attack can create new ones. Despite the obvious genital differences, men and women have more in common regarding where and when it is okay to touch than we may think; he has no-go areas just as she has, even though he may seek touch more urgently and less warily. And there will always be individual no-go areas: particularly sensitive regions, such as ankles or testes; tickle-spots such as ribs or feet; or scar tissue that remains vulnerable or tender.

Body-talk fluency undeniably means understanding both our own and our partner's no-go areas. When touch approaches we may feel tense, uncomfortable, suddenly cold, with all passion draining away. If we try to touch a partner's no-go area, we may sense holding-back signals, such as literally keeping that part of the body protected, edging back or using a hand to turn us away. Movement will slow down or stop, as may breathing, as a partner holds still until we move on to a safer part of the body.

Whether it is we who are wary or our partner who is tense, the best way to react to a pull-back is to respect it, both physically and emotionally. Steer clear of that spot on this occasion, and

Below. For many couples, the first foray inside clothes is a key stage, signalling progress to hitherto no-go areas. This is the time to be especially wary of any second thoughts, and to be willing to talk them through should they arise.

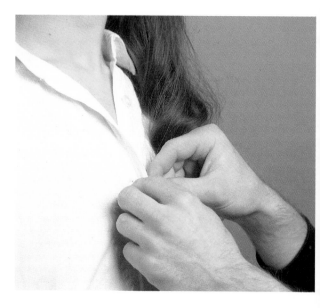

make it very clear that you are doing so, or your love-making will end in disaster.

Later, use the body talk of touch and closeness to signal safety and regain trust. Explain or explore together whether this no-go area is just for now, or is for ever. If for ever, be reassured that a no-go area is not a rejection of the other person, but simply a deep-rooted fear. If the no-go area is only temporary, return to it when trust and passion are more established.

Of course, the converse of no-go areas are those places that we particularly like to have touched. Erogenous zones (*see* pages 64–65), genital areas and comfort zones (*see* page 46) are key ones, but many of the places where we particularly want to be touched by a lover are just our own special areas that respond best to touch. By cradling a lover's head, stroking hair or massaging feet we learn particular go areas and delight in paying them attention.

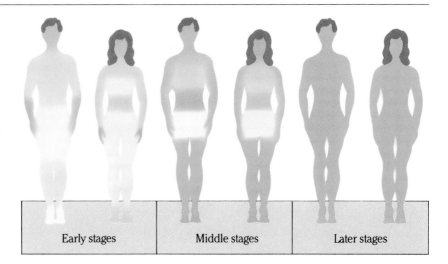

| Early stages | Middle stages | Later stages |

Right. The early stages of intimacy allow touching with the mouth (shown by the darker tone) on his lower arms, face and neck. For her, mouth touching on face and hands only is permissible. But touching by hand (shown by the lighter tone) is acceptable on his upper body and lower legs; her waist, shoulders and arms. In the middle stages, all parts of the body except the genitals are touchable by hand, although the increased intimacy of mouth contact is more limited. When full sexual contact is allowed, even the genitals are touchable, though whether or not mouth contact is made is still subject to individual desires or ihibitions.

Above. For many couples, go and no-go areas vary according to whether they are in the public gaze. The position of her hand shows not only that they have progressed beyond the first stage of intimacy, but that he likes to be touched there in public, and she is happy to be seen being so intimate.

Left. This couple appears to be closely connected, their faces nearly touching, her breasts against his chest. But look lower; while his pelvis is vertical, hers is tilted sharply away, signalling that she is not yet ready for further contact, or is pulling back from past intimacy. We then notice that in the upper half of the picture, his head is angled persuasively, while her direct gaze and back tension suggest an imminent confrontation.

UNDRESSING IN STYLE

Whether we are taking off our own clothes, or whether we are removing each other's, we should do it in style.

The way in which a partner removes his or her clothes, or strips us, tells us a great deal. A hasty, efficient removal probably means eagerness for love-making; although a slow, seductive one may well mean a more sensuous time is in store once passion begins. A partner who luxuriates in the feel of the clothes and in the sliding sensation as they reveal skin is a person who revels in touch; this will show in love-making. A partner who takes particular care and pride when revealing one part of his or her body certainly derives pleasure from that part and probably wants it to be touched and appreciated. Significant too is the way in which partners are focussed as they strip. Externally-focussed undressing, with lots of eye contact, attention to a partner and displaying movements will probably signify a confident or extrovert lover. Internally-focussed undressing may reveal shyness or uncertainty about what is to come, or simply that the person is uncomfortable about display.

When it comes to being stripped by a partner, people also vary in their response. Some hate to lose control by being undressed and will flinch away. The best response here is to draw back immediately, leaving your partner in control until he or she is ready to surrender it. Others revel in being waited on hand and foot. He is especially likely to lie back, hands behind head, and enjoy not having to act; she can first undress him and then move sensually up his body with kisses. If a partner indicates non-verbally a need to be undressed, it is particularly pleasurable to pander to this. Some people may find that this is the only time that they can relinquish control and be looked after.

Some women will sink into an almost child-like passivity, and love being undressed piece by piece while doing absolutely nothing. She may even lose her desire while being cared for. Try cuddling her if she does this, and leaving the sensuality for a while until she feels more aroused; she may be signalling with her body talk that she simply wants to be looked after rather than pleasured on this occasion.

Undressing can also be an opportunity for a 'rough-and-tumble', with both partners fighting to get each other's clothes off. If she resists when he tries to remove her clothes, she may be asking him to pretend to strip her forcefully. Hold her wrists down and take off her clothes one piece at a time, with delicate arousal in between, not trying to tease her but making this an erotic experience. If he resists, he will need to do so gently so that she is able to 'overpower' him. Of course, if a partner resists seriously, with angry voice or wary, averted gaze, he or she may be serious. Stop immediately, and check before going on; you may be encroaching on deep fears or distressing memories.

Undressing never has to be silent to be sensual. If you are unsure of how to set about undoing bra straps, suspenders, flies or braces, then ask your partner what you should do. A loving word to break the silence as both of you struggle with zips can release tension and bring you even closer together.

If we really wish to improve our technique for undressing, then practice makes perfect. A mirror can help, either before the act when we can try out different movements and gestures in front of it, or during the act to add extra piquance. Go slowly. Try removing clothes on the extremities first progressing to the final, genital-revealing essentials. Alternatively, reverse the process and begin with the genitals first: the sight of pubic hair or an erect penis peeping from beneath a garment can be very arousing.

Use flirting techniques (*see* pages 28–29),

They move slowly and sensuously towards nudity. Perhaps they are new lovers, or perhaps there is an uncertainty about each other's needs. His shirt is already unbuttoned, and he now turns his attention to her. They keep eye contact, their bodies angled towards each other, as he delicately unbuttons her blouse. Her smile tells him that she is very happy with what is happening, and her hand on his knee and arm on his back maintain contact. Their undressing is respectful and gentle rather than hasty and urgent; their love-making will almost certainly begin delicately, though as both gain confidence, they may move on to deeper passion.

alternating externally-focussed, revealing movements with slight drawing-back, hiding gestures. But remember that, if either you or your partner is embarrassed by displaying, then it is best to avoid flirting and to concentrate simply on being close and intimate as you undress. You can also try undressing each other with eyes closed, concentrating totally on tactile sensations and sounds, such as indrawn breaths or soft whispers of love, that tell you when your actions are working. There are very few more effective techniques of foreplay than really sensuous and stylish undressing.

EXPLORATION

Here is a list of dos and don'ts for taking off clothes.

● Do

Wear suspenders, but only if they turn you on too

Touch a great deal when undressing each other

Leave some clothes on sometimes

Experiment with undressing each other

Provide snug dressing gowns for after love-making

● Don't

Leave your socks until last

Struggle with her bra strap – ask for help

Rush things – undressing should be savoured

Wear ageing or very unfashionable underwear

Expect to get his jeans off without a struggle

AN EROGENOUS INVENTORY

Some parts of our body tend to give us more pleasure than others. Our genitals are obvious pleasure points. Yet we may sometimes forget that the rest of our body also has a capacity for arousal.

Our erogenous zones are key areas that particularly respond to sensual contact, signalling our readiness and preparing us for love-making. With arousal, blood capillaries come to the surface in these parts, making nerves more sensitive, swelling areas such as lips and ear lobes, increasing the surface available for touch.

To discover our erogenous zones, we can take an inventory by searching for where arousal is greatest. In holding back deliberately from full intercourse, we can take the time to discover our pleasure points. In so doing, we will gain knowledge that will stand us in good stead for our entire sexual life. Set aside three or four

Below. The shaded areas on these diagrams show some typical erogenous zones. His zones are focussed more around the genitals, while hers are spread more widely all over her body.

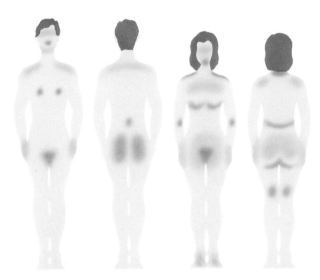

EXPLORATION
You may want to use the diagrams *above* as a template. After taking your inventory, mark in on the body shape your erogenous zones and how you like to be touched. Mark with different coloured pens the areas that are 'Mmmm', those that are 'Yes please', and those that are 'Oh, yes, yes, yes'.

Left. He brushes back her hair with his hand. While doing this, he is also exploring whether kissing, licking or biting her ear is most pleasurable for her.

Right. A particular touch on the side of her neck sends her wild; but he is discovering that, to produce the desired effect, the touch needs to be gentle rather than firm.

Right. He finds out whether nipples are erogenous zones for her and if so, how they respond to his touch.

Far right. Some areas sheltered from normal touch, such as inside of arm or back of knee, can be exquisitely sensitive.

Left. They hug before beginning to explore each other's body. Her head relaxes on to his shoulder gaining warmth and comfort, and she is beginning to sense his smell and taste.

hours with your partner in a warm, comfortable setting with a firm surface, floor or bed on which one of you can lie and the other can move freely. You are creating here a sensual rather than a sexual atmosphere with low lights and soft, relaxing music. Spend a while talking quietly, just being together, looking and listening, undressing each other gently and carefully.

Agree in advance any no-go areas. To make the inventory really work, agree that strictly genital areas (vagina and penis) are off-limits. Agree too – and this is vital – that intercourse will not happen until both inventories have taken place, and both of you have had your turn. Otherwise, someone will feel cheated.

One partner lies down, relaxing and focussing internally, then spends the next half hour discovering his or her own body sensations. The goal is to become more aware than ever before of what is good and what is not so good; what sensations are felt: hot or cold; tense or relaxed; moist or dry; tingly or static. He or she may also want to become aware of personal memories, thoughts or feelings, pictures or sounds that come to mind while becoming aroused.

The other partner can now begin to touch. The aim is to not to seduce into love-making, but to give as much pleasure as possible in as many ways as possible, finding as many erogenous zones as you can. You may begin with the seemingly least-sensitive areas – back, calves, thighs, feet, arms and hands – then move on to face, neck, chest, breasts and stomach.

Movements can vary. Resist the temptation to press firmly and steadily; such massage aims to relax and this inventory is about arousal. So use fingers and palms of hands, feet and eyelashes in all kinds of touch talk. Use mouth and tongue in all kinds of mouth music. Try feathers, massage oil, fur or velvet, or even (warn your partner first) the thrill of ice or the slither of cream.

Look, listen, feel. How is your partner responding? What can you hear from the breath or murmurs? What does the feel of the muscles and skin tell you? Stop immediately if something does not work; if something is good, stay with it for a while, then move on.

Afterwards, when time is up and your partner has emerged from a sensual haze, talk through what was best. Then it is your turn.

HER BREASTS

No two breasts are ever the same, even when they belong to the same woman. Some are big, some small, some firm and some soft. The left breast, curiously, is often larger than the right. Some nipples are constantly erect, some constantly inverted, some like raspberries, others small and flat. The areola around the breast can be tiny and neat, or spread out widely from the nipple, dark as chocolate or light as strawberry ice cream. Sometimes there are hairs growing round the nipple, sometimes there are scars that make the breast a mountain landscape.

In body-talk terms, breasts are an encyclopaedia of what a woman feels. To begin with, she will have feelings about her breasts, and perhaps these feelings will not all be positive. Convinced that they are too small, too big, too bouncy or too floppy, she may show this by her movements, curling her body inwards to hide her breasts. If she does this, support her. She may, in the trust of the moment, hold herself upright, shoulders back and head up, presenting her breasts; in this case, celebrate her.

He will have feelings about breasts too. His own may be sensitive and arousable, particularly the nipples. Hers may fascinate and arouse him, or may create in him feelings of childlike dependence. If he licks and sucks, quietly and without passion, he may be contacting early feelings and needs holding rather than sexuality. If he takes no notice at all of breasts, then he either gets no pleasure from them, or he has had a series of partners whose breasts were not for touching. He needs encouragement.

As she gets aroused, her breasts will almost certainly reflect this: fuller, redder, the nipples erect and engorged, the areola swelling as blood flows in. These signs of arousal are undeniable; her body is responding. The myth, however, is that these signs are always signals of pleasure within the breast itself. Many women gain immense pleasure from their breasts, reporting all-over arousal, intense sensation around the nipple, a direct sensual link between genitals and breasts. Others, however, receive no sensation: their erogenous zones are elsewhere.

How can we communicate what breasts need? Natural movements to gain contact are a pushing forward, a rubbing against, a turning of the body so that breasts are not forgotten in the heat of the moment. If they are, move a hand (or a head, or a penis) gently in the right direction.

How can we give breasts what they need? If she ignores them, then he probably can too, concentrating instead on her other erogenous zones. If her breasts want attention, be inventive. Learn from her own body talk; get her to put fingers on breasts, with your fingers over them, then learn the speed, pressure and rhythm of her movements. Watch her if she touches her breasts when aroused, and try copying her movements yourself. Experiment with mouth music, sucking and licking in different patterns, never biting unless she likes it. Remember that, like a penis, a nipple may need moisture to respond.

Be wary if your partner's attitude to breasts differs from your own. He may be wild about them, she a little uncertain; he may need nurturing from them, she may see them as pure pleasure. When mismatches occur, treat them gently: breasts are so precious they are bound to create strong emotion.

EXPLORATION
Let her complete this sentence in her own way, drawing inspiration from these suggestions:
I like to have my breasts... stroked lightly, teased, scratched, circled, massaged, licked, tongued, sucked, nibbled, blown on... with fingers, mouth, tongue, penis, something else... lightly/firmly, regularly/irregularly, roughly/smoothly... and as I get aroused, this varies in the following way...

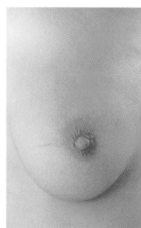

Above. Breasts change from day to day and week to week. At times, they can be soft and malleable; at other times, hard, swollen and granular. Just before and during a woman's monthly period, they may be particularly firm and rounded and also unusually vulnerable, or exquisitely sensitive.

Left. She covers herself with her arm, unsure. Her lowered head and solemn mouth reflect the movement. Before she can even begin to feel good, she needs loving touch and reassurance.

HER GENITALS

To understand really what our body says, we have to be familiar with our own, and our partner's genitals: what they are, what they do and how they communicate with us.

Begin by looking and touching. He can include this in a loving exploration of her body, while she can use a mirror to see herself fully. As part of love play, this can bring a sense of wonder to what may up to now have been a taboo area.

You will find, as you approach her genitals, that her mound of Venus is covered with pubic hair, maybe echoing her natural colouring, but thicker, shorter, curlier and sparser than her head hair. Parting the outer labia of her genitals, you will find the inner lips, in many different colours, with varying textures, possibly glistening with moisture. You will be able to see the ridge dividing this area from her anus, and then, the entrance to her vagina. Perhaps, still visible, will be the edges of her hymen and, unless she has been castrated, above that will be her clitoris.

Now begin to touch. Explore with gentle fingers her entire genital area. Be aware of how the outer and inner lips have different textures, how the moisture and warmth of the genitals varies as you touch it, how the vagina opens to your finger. Inside, notice the strength of the vaginal muscles, the difference in texture and sensation between the different sides of the vagina, and perhaps even – if she allows deep finger penetration – how the vagina ends in the cervix, the entrance to the womb. Find out too if she has the elusive (possibly mythical) G spot, the point on the front wall of the vagina that is said to be particularly sensitive and to 'ejaculate' on orgasm.

Then touch her clitoris. Notice its similarity to

Left. Her sensations rise as touch approaches her genitals. She may well feel this deep inside her vagina, right up to her diaphragm and out to her breasts, right down her thighs to the backs of her knees. Almost certainly there will be some centralized sensation deep in her core, in her clitoris or even round her anus. And there may be an answering response in all her erogenous zones: lips, ears, neck, insides of elbows and knees. She may describe her feelings as warm and tingling, as soft and melting, or as sharp and stretched out. Whatever, these sensations will build and build as she becomes more aroused.

EXPLORATION

She may want to think through these questions alone or to talk them through with him. Whichever, the answers will help both understand her body talk.

- What is the first thing you feel in your genitals when you are aroused and where do you feel it?
- How could you describe the sensations and what do they remind you of?
- Do you think of any images or sounds as your genitals begin to be aroused?
- How do these elements change as desire deepens?

Below. Knowing how her internal genital area is structured can help you to understand what happens on the outside. The lips (labia) of her vagina give way to her hymen which opens into her vagina. Beyond the cervix her uterus is ready for child-bearing; this can occur as a result of sperm from his ejaculation travelling to her ovary to fertilize the eggs there. When love-making, all these areas respond with increased sensitivity and arousal.

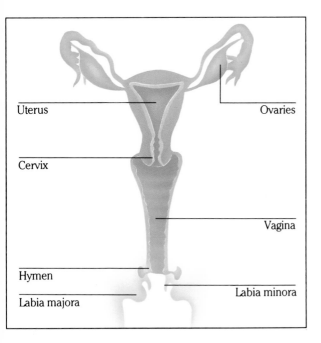

Uterus

Ovaries

Cervix

Vagina

Hymen

Labia majora

Labia minora

the penis – the two emerged from the same root organ when sexuality was determined in the womb – giving the clitoris a sensitivity and arousal rate that can equal and exceed that of its male equivalent. Slip back, if you can, the foreskin-like hood from the glans-like tip, to run your finger along the shaft, noticing how its tiny ridge of muscle runs below the skin's surface.

Notice her moisture, the texture and colour of her internal fluids and how they smell and taste. Some women only moisten a little, but unless she is ill or has a hormone imbalance, she should have some lubrication in her vagina. Notice how this changes as each month progresses and her period approaches and then passes.

Keep in mind what happens internally as she becomes aroused. Imagine how her entire uterus expands and lifts, opening her vagina wide and drawing her inner and outer lips apart, filling them with blood, increasing their sensitivity and flooding them with moisture. And then, if she is beginning to feel desire, learn how you can chart this arousal from the outside, using your senses to tell just what she feels. For it is a myth that, lacking an obvious erection, women show few signs of excitement. Their body talk is more subtle than a man's, but just as noticeable to a loving, knowledgeable partner. Each woman's signals will vary, but learning them is easy: simply look, taste, smell and touch.

Look for the labia blushing, swelling and opening out. Check genital odour, for her vagina will signal, by a subtle change, a two-step move from non-arousal to arousal and then to readiness for orgasm. The touch of your hand can gauge her clitoris hardening and engorging. Your finger inside her vagina may feel it dilate, plump up, contract and pull at your finger. Chart too her arousal through her fluids. Vaginal fluid is her body's way of signalling a move towards love-making, though the presence of moisture alone is no guarantee she is ready for intercourse.

All these signals may not be apparent at once. It will take time and loving attention truly to discover her genitals, and particularly to find out when they are ready for love-making.

HIS GENITALS

His genitals may seem all too easy to explore. In fact they are just as complex and subtle as hers. And in many ways, they are far more vulnerable, both physically and emotionally.

As with her, exploration could be part of a celebration of his body as she looks and touches it. He may feel he already knows his genitals well, but self-exploration in a loving, sexual context may be something he has never done before.

His non-erect penis is small and perhaps slightly crumpled. It can, like her clitoris, vary in shape, size and colour. The skin, like hers, comes in different shades and textures, with the cone-shaped glans smoother and shinier, and at its base the ridge of the corona.

Circumcision – the removal of the foreskin – is one of the oldest human rituals. It prevents dirt getting trapped within the foreskin. Some believe that circumcision heightens his potential for arousal, and delays orgasm. Others suggest that, as the foreskin is retracted anyway during love-making, it makes no difference.

Below the penis, hanging between his legs, are the testicles, his equivalent of her ovaries. One is often smaller than the other, hangs lower than the other or disappears, retreating into the warm comfort of his body. Behind the testicles is the muscular circle of the anus, often sensitive to the touch as well, and capable of pleasure when he is aroused.

Having looked, now touch. How do the foreskin and the skin around his testicles feel? As you touch, watch for the responding movement, as the penis begins to come erect. As it fills with blood, the muscles around it contract, preventing the blood from leaving, turning the limp organ into an uprisen one. Again, size varies, and an erect penis can be thick, thin, narrow, wide or even slightly asymmetric.

You can feel as well as see the huge changes that erection brings: the hardness, strength and

Right. For him, the stirring of his erection may be the very first sensation that makes him fully aware of his own desire and arousal. Whilst he may have sensations of warmth and comfort all over his body, he is likely to feel the most intense sensation at the tip of his penis, or possibly in his testes. He may constantly be acutely aware of his erection, of how it dips and rises, and this will both affect and be affected by his love-making; equally, once stimulated, he will often be able quickly and easily to meet the demands of his own desire.

EXPLORATION

He may choose to think through these questions alone; or to talk them through with her.
- What is the first thing you feel in your genitals when you are aroused and where do you feel it?
- How could you describe the sensations and what do they remind you of?
- Do you think of any images or sounds as your genitals begin to be aroused?

Below. His penis ends in the glans with the ridge of the corona at its base and the prepuce or foreskin intact or circumcised. Running the length of the penis is the urine-carrying urethra that discharges from the tip of the penis. The testicles are contained in the pouch of the scrotum; the vas deferens carries the sperm from the testicles to the penis.

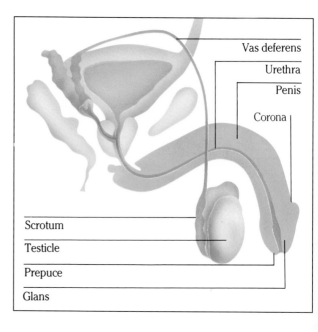

Vas deferens

Urethra

Penis

Corona

Scrotum

Testicle

Prepuce

Glans

movement of the penis. As it rises, you may see the contraction that brings the testicles closer to the body, and the movement of the foreskin, ready to expose the sensitive glans.

What changes can you see in the colour of his penis as the blood fills it, or the testicles as they shift? Watch the veins on his penis stand out and trace their contours with a finger. Feel, smell and taste the tiny drops of moisture that may gather at the penis end.

All these signs are clear and unmistakeable, very different from the hidden secrets of the vagina. And hence the myth that an erection is a simple thing, needing no subtlety, care or attention. The knowledgeable lover knows differently. For if her vulnerability is that her arousal is not obvious, his is that his arousal, or lack of it, is all too obvious. So he may worry that he is not firm enough, believing that hard erection is the key to giving satisfaction. There is an answer. By learning to read the subtle signals of his genital body talk, both of you can learn to respond to the exact state of his erection. Loving attention to body talk will enable you both to respond, even when he is feeling insecure about his potency. But do not fall into the trap of concentrating on his erection to the exclusion of all else. Remember too to show his genitals loving care and attention, even when they are not directly aroused. Men, more so than women, may focus on their genitals as the source of pleasure, but they often see pleasure as only possible with erection; he may sometimes need reminding that his genitals can be loved even when they are not in action.

Chapter Three
MAKING LOVE WORK

We are now ready to move on to true sexuality, the peak of our physical relationship. By trusting each other enough to merge bodies as well as minds and emotions, we take the final step to true intimacy.

Without body-talk skills to help us, this final step is sometimes when we feel most distanced from our partner. We may have no way of knowing what is wanted or of showing what we desire, and love-making can be the loneliest activity in the world if we are not truly communicating. If we have never learned how to demonstrate our own needs or to read our partner's signals we may find that we withdraw into seeking only our own pleasure. A full knowledge of body talk is therefore more vital then ever at this stage, for it allows us fully to contact each other through the varied movements of love, deeply alive to every nuance of movement and touch.

And so we begin love-making, perhaps trusting our partner enough to reveal how we pleasure ourselves, then gaining the knowledge to pleasure our partner by hand or mouth. Then, perhaps, we move into full sexual intercourse, learning from the dance of penetration the ways we like to move, and the positions we like to take to achieve the height of pleasure. We reach out for orgasm and, once it comes, it draws us even closer together. Afterwards, we learn how to relax together in a way that renews our intimacy. With every touch, sensation, movement and response, we are learning more about each other as we go along, and we are building love.

They fully communicate on all levels as they lovingly move closer.
Her peaceful expression and closed eyes show that she is concentrating
totally on what she feels, sensing the muscles of his back and waist under her
hands. His hands meanwhile both support and comfort, as his body touches
hers down its whole length. They breathe with each other, smell and
taste each other as they prepare for love-making.

SEXUAL TIMING

Right. Arousal times (1) differ in length, before erection (2) of his penis and her clitoris signals the beginning of movements towards orgasm (3), followed by relaxation (4). *Far right.* The solid line shows that she may be left frustrated (5) if he climaxes without regard for her sexual timing.

We each progress differently through the stages of love-making. Our body responds slowly or quickly, our mind leaps forward or holds back. We pass through each step – foreplay, erection, point of no return, orgasm – at varying rates and with different levels of enthusiasm.

For her, the pace can be slow. The process can begin, in fact, many hours before actual love-making, when with sight and sound, touch and smell, she begins to become aware of her sensual and sexual arousal. Then, a long period of foreplay, both emotional and physical, may involve extended, sensuous body touching, and closeness to her partner, experiencing him on every level. She will almost certainly need lengthy care and attention to her clitoris, breasts, buttocks and other erogenous zones. If love-making involves penetration, this may mean her arousal dips and she needs to build up again to her climax. When it comes, however, her orgasm may be followed by another, her capacity for love-making undimmed. She will often be able to stay aroused for hours at a time.

For him, it may be very different. His erection makes him ready to move now; he may like, but hardly needs, any other stimulation and, once aroused, he can move towards orgasm immediately. Inside vagina, hand or mouth, his urgent desire will be to move, to thrust, to reach orgasm. Often he can do this within minutes; often he will have to hold back consciously in order not to orgasm within a very short space of time. Once over the point of no return, his climax will signal a need for immediate rest. He may

His typical sexual timing

Her typical sexual timing

How the timings often fail to meet

take several hours to become aroused again.

How can we move these very different cycles to match? For while it is often the man who takes the lead, it is also he whose sexual cycle is briefest; his leadership may leave her abandoned half-way through her cycle, and frustrated. She meanwhile may seem to be holding him back; he may need to struggle to stem his arousal.

The answer is not simply being able to climax easily or being able to delay. The issue is not about orgasm alone, but about the whole love-making process. Knowing body talk, we can calibrate all the signs we now know – sight, sound, moisture, smell, and taste – to gauge our partner's arousal. We can develop further our sexual codes to communicate infallibly what we want when we want it. We can use our

Above. This love-making sequence shows that, by matching timings, prolonging his arousal and erection (1 and 2, dotted line) and hers (1 and 2, solid line), her final orgasm and his climax (3) can match and synchronize before relaxation (4).

EXPLORATION
Draw a diagram, like the ones *above*, of your ideal sexual timing. Get your partner to do the same. Then compare them. What mismatches are there? How could you communicate them to each other, and avoid them next time you make love?

knowledge to stay in each stage and move on from it at the right time for both of us. We can synchronize our timing and our approach, our reactions and our responses so that both of us get the pleasure we want, all the time.

SHOWING YOUR PARTNER HOW

If we really want our partner to know what we like, then there is an easy way in which we can achieve this: demonstration.

We may need to begin by talking, sharing fears or worries together. Love-making is such a mutual joy that to take our passion separately, with our partner not acting but watching, can be a fearful thing, so share your concerns. If you are worried that your way of masturbating will seem strange to your partner, say so. If your partner is concerned that you might want to masturbate more than to make love, then give reassurance. Agree in advance that whoever is masturbating can take as much time as is required – and can stop at any point if feelings of embarrassment should arise of if arousal should disappear. You may even want to begin in the dark, working up slowly to watching each other.

Then, indulge yourself. This is your time, and you can organize it in any way you want. Arrange the setting just as you like it, so you are lying, sitting or even standing in the right way for you. Add cushions, oil or any other props that you need. Ask your partner to sit or lie in a supportive way, within reach. If you want, touch and kiss each other and get your partner to arouse you until you are ready to focus inwards and pleasure yourself .

When you are ready, take it slowly. Do not expect to feel at ease immediately; you may need to giggle a bit before you are comfortable with your partner watching. When you do begin to feel aroused, concentrate on that. Make your focus internal; this is a time to pay attention not to your partner, but to yourself. Pleasure yourself completely and in your particular way, rubbing and stroking, holding back or moving on, until you have done all you want and are ready to stop. Then, take from your partner what you need: this may be a cuddle; more kissing; help in reaching orgasm; intercourse or simply some time spent lying quietly together.

If you are the watcher, your role is a dual one You are there for your partner, offering support when it is needed. But you are learning as well. You are learning directly how to please your partner in a way he or she may never have experienced before, for perhaps no one has ever taken the trouble to learn what his or her intimate body talk is saying. This is the time when, with no other distractions, you can simply watch, listen and attend to every signal your partner gives about what is liked and what gives the most pleasure.

As your partner prepares to masturbate, look particularly for what is important about the setting. Is a support being used to raise the body or pelvis? What position does your partner need to take: lying; sitting or standing; on the back or on the front? Notice how touch is carried out: with the hand; by pressing thighs together; with a cushion; using fingers to penetrate vagina or anus or using the other hand to stroke testicles. And exactly where does your partner need to be touched: the tip of the penis; the depths of the vagina; the shaft of the clitoris? You may need to check this by asking your partner to let you trace how his or her fingers are placed. Does he need to pull his foreskin back, and how does he do this? Does she pull her labia apart or ease the hood of her clitoris back?

Then look at the type of movement your partner uses: what pressure; what speed; and particularly, what variation? Does he stop and start; does she hold herself back; does he thrust with his pelvis; does she slide her fingers back and forth?

Watch all this while listening for the sounds, words, murmurs and breathing that let you calibrate when arousal rises and when it pauses. What do such noises tell you about the right rhythm or even mood for stimulation?

EXPLORATION

Take the time, maybe with your partner, to think about what you really like when you masturbate yourself.

- What position do you need to be in?
- Do you need any props?
- What do you use to touch yourself: hand; fingers; something else?
- What movement; pressure; speed; rhythm?
- What variations in each of these?
- How moist do you need to be?
- Now try to answer these questions for your partner.

Afterwards, talking it through is vital for both of you. Share your delight in how you felt and what you saw while your partner was masturbating and also discuss what you experienced. Give reassurance that she did not look ugly when she came, or that he did not look stupid when he masturbated. Experiment, showing each other how to touch, how to move, how to stop or start to have the most effect. Ask questions, offer suggestions, check whether what is good in masturbation would also work in intercourse. Above all, learn how what works for one can also work for two.

It can be difficult to feel at ease when masturbating in front of a partner; we often think our pleasure is unimportant and that we need to hurry back to real love-making. In watching you masturbate, your partner may not only be learning ways to love you but may also find the experience arousing.

PLEASURING HER

Pleasuring your partner takes body-talk knowledge and skill. As you masturbate her, remember first what you learned when you explored her genitals and when you watched her masturbate herself. Recall the hardening of her clitoris, the moisture of her vagina, the facial expressions of passion, the sound codes that meant she was approaching her orgasm, the patterns of movement and rhythm that you learned she desired.

Then add the knowledge you can only gain by action rather than observation. When you masturbate her, use all your knowledge to touch her in a way that you know she will find pleasing, but check constantly whether what you are doing is working. If you are using your hand, you can watch her, checking her expression, her colour change, the way her stomach tenses or her face flushes; if you are using your tongue, you will be able to taste and smell her responses. Let her

Left. She takes her pleasure while he focusses all his attention on her, and puts all his efforts into satisfying her needs. Her eyes are closed as she moves into an internal space full of her own pictures, memories, sounds and feelings. Her hands on her chest are ready to move to her already aroused breasts if she needs to stimulate herself further.

EXPLORATION
What do you really like when your partner masturbates you and how does this vary according to whether he uses his hand, mouth, penis or another part of his body?
● What position do you need to be in?
● What movement; pressure; speed; rhythm?
● What variations in each of these?
● How moist do you need to be?
● What else do you need and like when he is masturbating you?
● How does what you like vary during arousal?
● How does what you like from your partner differ from the way you like to masturbate yourself?

noises and breathing guide you. You may be able to feel the response of the clitoris and the clutching movement of the vagina as well as her body shifting under you as she moves.

Start by checking that her body is signalling that she is comfortable, relaxed and ready to begin; if she fidgets or wriggles away, move with her to the right position. Could you, by touching her breast, stroking her hair, holding her hand or leaning over her in a particular way, create the extra arousal that she wants?

Then start to touch her. When using your hand, try the whole palm or single fingers. Trace the movements she used when you watched her pleasuring herself. When using your tongue, you have fewer precedents to go on, though you may like to try imitating the tongue movements she uses when she kisses. For both, calibrate her pelvic movements as she responds to you. And it is important to remember that her needs may vary from day to day and hour to hour, so expect to take a while to get to know her repertoire of preferences.

If she suddenly or gradually ceases moving or silences her noise, she may be losing her arousal. If so, move back to an early stage, such as cuddling and kissing, or to early movements that you know were good, as you start to pleasure her again.

Experiment with different types and patterns of stroke; alternate fast and slow finger movements, and a soft and erect tongue. Move from clitoris to labia, to vagina and back again. Renew her moisture constantly unless she prefers it dry, dipping a finger into her vagina to transfer genital

Below. Her hand over his allows her to guide him, controlling the pressure of his fingers, and the speed and pace of his movements. In this way, she is very much in charge of her own sensations. She can stop him as she reaches the point of no return, allowing him to start again as the pleasure begins to dim in order to keep her hovering on the brink for hours.

juices, or providing the saliva yourself. Remind yourself of the rhythm she likes and expect her to correct you until you get it right. Does she prefer solid, steady pressure or delicate, light, unrhythmical movement? Stop and start if that is what she showed you, but you will probably find that it is usually better to shift to a regular, heavy rhythm as she nears her climax. Be prepared to touch more of her body and speak words of love to her as she begins to orgasm.

PLEASURING HIM

When pleasuring him, do not be distracted by the myths. He might not want rough movement all of the time; and he does not necessarily need penis-centred loving. He may want to be stroked gently, kissed softly or licked lovingly. There are no rules.

And as there are no rules, you have to use your own intuition and his body talk. You will know by now what he looks like when he is aroused, how his voice changes and his body feels when he is lost to passion. Now learn to distinguish the grades of erection, the slightest changes in skin colour, the minutest shifts in breathing. Let him tell you when what you are doing is right, and when it could be better.

A movement of his hand or a shift of his body will tell you that he wants you at his penis. Perhaps he guides your head down or perhaps you know when, from his languorous state, he wants to be the receiver rather than doer. The sigh of relaxation as you move down his body will tell you that you have guessed right.

Once there, you have help, an unmistakeable signal of his exact state of arousal. His erect penis will have a number of positions at various angles up and down the scale; from this you can calibrate just how to make your next move.

You will have learned from watching him how he likes his penis to be held; experiment, knowing that if you need to, you can return to this preferred position. Retract the foreskin if he likes that, then move with enthusiasm. Delicately caress his penis between your lips then take it deep into your mouth; circle a finger and thumb around the corona; use one hand or two; put one hand on his testicles; use no hands at all just a firm mouth; and place his penis between your breasts or anywhere it feels good to him. Check for his reaction at every stage.

Experiment, as always, with speed, pressure, rhythm and movement. Try varying the speed:

EXPLORATION
What do you really like when your partner masturbates you and how does this vary according to which part of her body she uses?
- What position do you need to be in?
- Do you need your foreskin up or retracted?
- What movement; pressure; speed; rhythm?
- What else do you need and like?
- How does what you like from your partner differ from the way you like to masturbate yourself?

slower; faster; making him wait. Move hands or fingers up and down, varying the pressure as they pass the corona. Rub the head of the penis on a moistened palm. Suck deeply or shallowly, lick like a lollipop, run your tongue around the glans, lick the shaft, lick the sensitive underside of the glans, take one testicle in your mouth. Try everything and see what works.

His whole body, its erotic tension, its total relaxation, or its bucking movement, will tell you whether to continue or to change direction. If he flinches even slightly, slow down and soften; not

all men like it rough. If his responding movement is firm and direct, try firming your own in answer, matching his energy with your own. If he lies quietly and simply moans, carry on.

Learn too, of course, from his penis, now fully firm with blood veins clearly touchable and a distinct deepening of colour. If what you are doing is good, you may feel minute surges of fluid up its shaft, raising it higher, and a shift in smell or taste as he passes pre-ejaculation moisture. And his testicles may be moving, shifting in response, changing in size, signalling with every touch that they enjoy being pleasured.

Check too what he needs on the rest of his body. Perhaps his nipples need fondling or his buttocks stroking. He may not feel able to touch himself so make contact with him. Rub your body over his, exchanging moisture and learning about his body tension. Reach up, as your hand keeps its rhythm, to kiss his mouth.

As he moves towards orgasm, go with him, using, hands, mouth and your whole body, finding the right movements and sounds to match his, lasciviously, all the way to climax.

Above. He guides her hand down to touch him intimately, then relaxes and lets her take the lead. She leans over to kiss him while her hand starts to move gently, in the first stages of bringing him to erection.

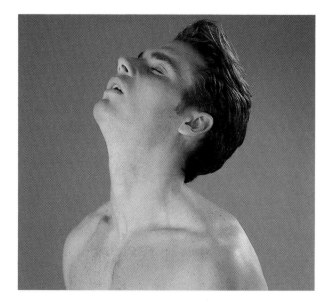

Above. All of his body-talk signals are telling her that he is aroused. Looking up from her arousal of his penis she can see his tension, open mouth and thrown-back head; from all this, she will deduce that his climax is not far away.

SIGNS TO PENETRATE

Penetration in love-making can be the height of sexuality. At its best, it can be a unique statement of oneness with our partner, an experience of mutual pleasure. But our readiness to move to penetration can vary. We can, from time to time and from context to context, fight shy of it or want to wait. How are we to know when the time is right? How can sexual body talk help us here?

His erection will be unmistakable, ready to thrust and move; he will imagine penetration and the feeling of warmth and moisture greeting him as he enters. She may feel her vagina hot or thrusting, wet and empty, wanting to be filled. Both may feel muscle spasms in their buttocks, a regular, rhythmic movement towards each other or a pressure between them that demands further contact.

He may shift, pulling her towards him, or easing her legs open, moving across or on top of her or just making tiny, unconscious movements towards doing each of these things. She will have already moved through all the stages of arousal and made or received reflective movements such as deep kissing and fingers penetrating her vagina. Her nipples may be erect and she may be moist, though neither of these signs alone are sufficient to signal her readiness for sexual intercourse. But if she pulls him towards her, puts her hands on his hips or buttocks or puts her hand down to guide his penis in, she is undoubtedly ready for penetration. She may push forward with mouth, tongue, breasts and pelvis. She may let her legs fall open, ready for him to move over and between them. Then, as the first move is made, there will be a change of speed, a slowing-down as they concentrate on penetration, a momentary renewal of conscious contact as they emerge from the depths of desire to move to intercourse. They may open their eyes, kiss briefly, lean back slightly to focus on

each other's face, confirming with this contact their aware decision to move into the final stage of intimate touch. As they do this, his erection may dip slightly and need to be helped in.

How can we calibrate when penetration is not yet right? His reservations will be more obvious: an erection falling as he pulls back or moves her hand away. She has fewer obvious signs of uncertainty, though a lack of moisture will, if she normally gets moist, tell both of them that she is not ready. But even when wet, she may signal uncertainty by moving back subtly, closing her legs slightly or simply letting her signs of arousal

Face to face, they kiss deeply, bodies entwined. Their movements against each other signal their readiness for penetration, her hand pulling him keenly towards her, his hand placed firmly on her buttocks.

Both partners draw back slightly from each other, their eye contact confirming that the next step is indeed one that they want to take. Her hand reaches down for him while he moves back to allow her room to do so.

lie. Either partner may shift the focus back to an earlier stage of foreplay, to the last point where needs did synchronize, gradually working up from there until it is time to try again.

When everything feels right, the moves are made and we achieve penetration. We will know it is right by its ease, as a penis will slide firmly inside a fully moist vagina. Our whole body responds to this movement with an immediate sense of relaxation, perhaps a deep, simultaneous release of breath or a momentary pause to enjoy the closeness. Then the arousing movements of intercourse can begin.

EXPLORATION
In which of the following ways do you signal to your partner that you are ready for intercourse? How does he or she signal this to you? In which of the following ways do you signal to your partner that you are *not* ready for intercourse? How does he or she signal this to you?
- Movement
- Reflective movement
- Nipple, penis or clitoral erection
- Movement of penis or tongue
- Tone of voice

His closed-mouth kiss marks a shift to a momentarily less passionate level as he prepares for penetration to take place. Her hand guides him further towards her and, as she does so, she starts to turn over onto her back.

His hand is outstretched to steady him as he rolls across and above her. She facilitates the move by placing a firm hand on his buttock, to keep him inside her as much as is possible now that penetration has begun.

Above her now, and firmly penetrating, he uses both hands to support his weight. Her legs open wide to receive him, her hands pull him towards her and both partners move together into an open-mouthed kiss.

She receives him deeply inside her, her knees raised to allow more penetration, her hands – still on his buttocks – pulling him further in. Her closed eyes and open mouth show her arousal as he begins to move.

SIGNS TO CHANGE POSITION

Position is important. With it, we can control the depth of penetration, allow different sensations on different parts of our genitals, give her the clitoral pleasure she needs, give him a swift and urgent orgasm, allow control, allow eye contact, give a little closeness, permit a little distance. How do we know which position to use? How do we know which is right just now and which should come next? Elegant body talk will provide the answer.

A position that is right is, quite simply, one that feels right. We will feel relaxed when we first move into it and, later, increasing sensations of pleasure in vagina, penis, and clitoris, with all-over body signals of arousal.

A position that feels wrong, either initially or during love-making, is signalled by discomfort, fading pleasure and signals of lost attention from both partners. Either or both may cease moving, turn away in discomfort, open their eyes or wriggle. Maybe he will begin to lose his rhythm or have to stop to ease the strain on shoulders or legs. Maybe she will find her sensations dying as her clitoris fails to be touched or the wrong part of her vagina is stimulated.

Perhaps the position is just too right, moving one or both of us inexorably towards an orgasm we do not yet want. Urgent moves – or a total stillness in a desperate attempt to control movement – may signal that a change of position is needed immediately unless intercourse is to climax within seconds.

If a position is wrong, we should change it. Our needs dictate the shift. If he needs more depth, perhaps indicating this by thrusting in or pulling her towards him, then the next step will be a position where her legs are up or curled round him. If she needs less penetration, signalling this by pulling away slightly or trying to slow the pace, then a rear or side-entry position could follow. If, as with many positions, clitoral stimulation is minimal, any position where the clitoris receives touch or body pressure would suit. And if we signal a need for eye contact by pulling back to look at our partner, then we need a position with some distance between us.

Who makes that move? It is still often he who takes the lead while she may signal her needs less obviously. Both will usually shift slightly in their chosen direction, check that the other is following, then move clearly together. Well performed, it is a dance, a miracle of power-steering with both bodies moving in unison, keeping rhythm and speed almost intact. Done without awareness, when one is pushing or the other resisting, the whole thing can grind to a halt with penis slipping from vagina. And sometimes, as with all intimacy, there is a real no, a genuine resistance by one to the non-verbal suggestion of the other. Perhaps one partner makes a grumbling sound, stops quite suddenly, turns over or away or emerges from passion to voice an objection.

Happily, though, there are positions for everyone. There are perhaps 100 to be found in sex manuals; most people, when they settle to a loving relationship, use two or three favourites. We could all experiment more, not for the sake of novelty, but simply because few positions meet every need, and many meet the needs of only one partner. Good lovers provide for a variety of moods and changing physical wants. Good lovers also extend their existing 'codes' to include signals about position. Try fingertip pressure to indicate a shift in direction, or a change in weight distribution to ease both of you over. Try a verbal code: murmurs to indicate a shift to left or right; an emphatic sound when the right place has been reached. In time, these codes will become part of natural love-making, and moving to the right position for both of you will become second nature.

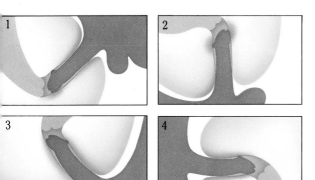

Left. The genital areas stimulated by different positions. (1) shows positions with him on top; (2) shows positions with her on top; (3) shows rear-entry positions. The most overall sensation is gained from the X position (4), where penetration is achieved by her sitting on his 'lap'.

EXPLORATION
Which of these four sexual positions do you enjoy sometimes; a great deal; not at all? What do you enjoy about them? What sensations do you feel?
● Missionary position; woman on top; penetration from behind; penetration from the side.

Above. She sits astride him leaning back, able to control depth of penetration by her position; he allows her to move.

Above. Both lean forward, able to touch and stroke each other; her clitoris can also touch or be touched with ease.

Above. Sitting, he can kiss her breasts while she cups his head; he holds her firm with his hands.

Below. Bent back, she takes the weight on her hands, while he adds extra sensation by kissing her breasts and stomach.

SIGNS TO CHANGE THE PACE

Main picture. Every sign here is for gentle, affectionate love-making, with her hand resting lightly but in control on his shoulder. *Inset.* Later, with her legs brought higher to allow penetration, he quickens the pace for more urgency.

Other than position, what variations can we give the dance of intercourse? Our speed can vary, from the slowest of movements to a fast, thrusting pace that builds inexorably to a climax. Our rhythm can alter, from a steady and regular beat to a broken and fitful one. Movements can stop and start to hold back and build up desire. The depth of the thrust can vary, sometimes deep into the very heart of the vagina, sometimes barely entering it. And the pressure of the thrust can vary too, from hard and sure to light and delicate.

With these variations, the simple in-and-out movement turns into a complex dance of pleasure. It can adapt to meet our needs moment by moment, perhaps beginning with light, delicate, shallow thrusts, moving through deeper, harder and faster thrusts until we climax. And although that pattern – from slow to fast, shallow to deep, light to hard – is the classic one, we can also use other patterns as the mood takes us. After hours of hovering deliriously on the brink, climax can result from the tiniest movement which sends us both tumbling over the edge. It can come, if we are ready, after just a few minutes of deep and powerful thrusting. It can also result from almost mathematical equations of movement: ancient Chinese sex manuals recommended formal combinations of fast and slow, deep and shallow thrusting in strict, numbered rotation.

So how do we tell what we need in order to climax? Our genitals signal to us what they want from moment to moment; if we can learn to read their signs we will be able to satisfy them. The only way, as always, is to experiment and find what pleases us; the only danger is to believe that hard, fast, deep and regular is the only way to thrust to orgasm.

From our partners we get clear signals too. Moving back, pulling away or shifting to earlier foreplay will often mean a need for slower, shallower, lighter movements. Pulling closer, pushing against us, squeezing or adding pressure will mean the opposite. Breathing that stops and starts may signal a need for teasing, unrhythmical thrusts. Look too for reflective signs, such as his light and slow kissing or the way she is pumping the penis as she holds it. If we look for our partner's natural rhythms (and not those they are using to please us), we may well find out the way our partner really likes to make love.

Sometimes it will be right to stop completely, not in distress, but simply to catch our breath. Then we realize a need for no speed, no rhythm, no depth and no pressure, but rather a hug, a smile and a glance before plunging back again into passion.

Above. Light, finger-tip touches keep the speed slow and gentle, showing her relaxed mood and her need for prolonged love-making. He can perhaps pause between thrusts to extend the pleasure.

Above. She quickens the pace with firmer stroking at the base of the spine. Perhaps she presses harder to gain better penetration and this may also increase his pace of movement.

Above. A firmer grip asks him for more depth and pressure, making him move even faster. She may use her fingernails to press into his buttocks, making further contact and urging him on.

COMING TOGETHER

Aiming to have mutual orgasms is a glorious goal. We should neither expect nor demand that we climax simultaneously – although we may welcome that if it happens – but we can work towards mutuality, a common commitment to each other's orgasm. And we should not be satisfied with a situation where one partner always climaxes and the other never does.

Firstly, a reminder about sexual timing (*see* pages 74–75). Mutual orgasm is not a question of love and luck. Even women who experience orgasm may take hours from first arousal to reach climax, while many men, particularly at the start of a new relationship, climax easily and within minutes. Most male and female timings to orgasm differ radically, so it is a wonder that we ever synchronize.

The second step is to use body talk. Can you spot when your partner is moving to orgasm? Can your partner learn to tell when you are reaching climax? If you can do this, you are half-way there.

Learn to sense patterns of passion, to distinguish the exquisitely subtle signals of difference in

During love-making, their body talk is very revealing. He nears his climax, while her open eyes and slumped body show her real emotional state.

arousal rates. Learn to tell when she is caught up in his desire, moving and crying with him but nowhere near her climax. Learn to know when he is moving ahead, almost at the point of no return, with thrusts speeding up and rising urgency. Learn to see when, from the outside, it looks like equal passion but, from the inside, it just feels wrong. Learn to recognize these things as soon as they happen, then act.

Act to move her on, act to slow him down. He can learn to spot the very first signals of his approaching orgasm, and immediately to withdraw, mentally or actually, from passion. Counting backwards from 100, or any similar concentrated mental exercise guaranteed to move his mind away from his penis, may work, though sometimes pulling out, accompanied by a loving touch, may be the only way.

She can take control here too. At the start she can slow him down, move him back into foreplay, take his attention from his penis by calling his name in a loving way. She can take responsibility for shifting gear if she senses he is moving more quickly than she is towards the peak: changing from oral sex to kissing or suggesting they take turns to arouse each other.

EXPLORATION
You and your partner already have ways to ensure that you move together through the stages of arousal. Think of three of those ways in which you synchronize the timing of your needs and desires. And yet there will be other ways in which you dance to a different tune during sex. Think of three new things you can do to help synchronize your timings even more.

Above. With good timing, his orgasm (the orange line) will coincide with her final climax (the shaded area).

Or, as crisis comes, she can squeeze his penis firmly, just on the corona. Three or four seconds should be enough to dim his arousal; when he is less erect, his breathing easier, his colour more normal, she can let go, and begin again.

For her, there are many ways to speed the process. Foreplay with all the attention on her may seem selfish, yet it can mean that penetration brings quick and easy orgasm for both. Spending enough time on her whole body, breasts and buttocks, her many erogenous zones and particularly her genitals, is vital. Let her be the one to say when she is ready for penetration, and let both partners realize that penetration may also reduce her desire by reducing effective stimulation, even if only momentarily. If this does happen, then look for ways to create that stimulation. At first, it may seem unspontaneous; with practice, it is as natural as intercourse. If she can orgasm through masturbation, then together he and she can find positions where she can equally well orgasm through sexual intercourse. Perhaps she needs a position that puts pressure on her clitoris or pulls it with each thrust. With her on top, either partner can reach to touch it. If she prefers to lie, then on her side or her front may give the same possibilities. Even with the missionary position, a hand slid down between bodies can often give enough stimulation to move her on. Remember too that orgasm does not need to happen only through full sexual intercourse; mutual masturbation with hand or mouth can even give simultaneous orgasms, though if either partner climaxes violently when giving oral sex, he or she may need to pull back a little to avoid causing possible injury to a lover's most sensitive parts.

As the peak arrives, through whichever route to orgasm, then keep communicating. It could be that something in particular could bring the orgasm a moment nearer or hold it off for a moment more. A loss of spontaneity, and a need to pause, experiment, and work back up again may occur when you first try this. But body talk soon may be able to make it a truly simultaneous, as well as mutual, orgasm.

ORGASM

The French call it 'little death', but in most love-making orgasm is the peak of living. Sensation builds; like a waterfall, the edge is inevitable and we plunge over it. For everyone, orgasm is different; it also varies at different times. Sometimes it will be a peaceful sigh; at other times, a volcano of sensation. He will probably feel it concentrated on his penis; she may know it as an all-body experience. If she experiences both clitoral and vaginal orgasms, then she may differentiate between the sensations they bring, the clitoral orgasm creating strong or over-sensation, the vaginal orgasm seeming to occur more deeply within her.

For both him and her, the experience differs with the kind of physical contact being made and with the timing: whether love-making has been short and sharp or an extended ecstasy of stopping and starting. And then there are multiple orgasms: continuous peaks that, at least so far, seem to be her possibility only. Repeated orgasms demand a gap between them for him, less so for her; extended orgasms last longer, the longest orgasm ever recorded lasted for 43 seconds.

What is needed during orgasm? Although we match each other more fully than ever before in heart-rate, breathing, and movement as each of us climaxes, our needs are different, even if subtly so. As always, matching touch with similar contact will work best. Desperate thrusting near climax will probably signify a need for hard, firm contact; she may want sudden, strong stimulation, often much firmer than was needed to bring her to the edge; and both he and she may need reassurance as orgasm approaches that the other is not going to stop. But experiment too with light touches on face, back or buttocks; these are often what is needed to complement the climax. And we should never forget sound: mutual gasps or moans, murmurs of love or shouts of ecstasy tipping pleasure over into orgasm.

Above. They move together slowly and rhythmically, holding on to each other as passion builds. Her vagina is becoming engorged with blood, his testicles begin to rise and his corona swells. Her hand on her breast arouses her still further.

Above. They begin to feel themselves move to the point of no return, their muscle tension showing clearly. Her vagina swells to grip his penis; his hard thrusts bring him fully erect. Perhaps a sex flush begins to show on their skin.

Above. She leans back, as they both slide into their climax. Her muscles begin to contract, while semen rushes up his shaft. Their breathing, blood pressure and heart-rate start to peak as they grip each other firmly.

Right. As they move together, her contractions spiral outwards from her pelvis to vagina; her erect clitoris may spasm too. His penis begins to ejaculate at the same rate, approximately four-fifths of a second apart.

Below. As his semen spurts into her, her vagina opens to receive it. They are at the peak of their orgasm, lasting from a few short spasms up to 15 seconds; their whole body responds to this climax of sensation.

EXPLORATION

What do you (or your partner) feel when you come? Describe the sensations you feel when you have your orgasm. Do these sensations vary according to how you have had your orgasm, or the kind of orgasm you have had? What do you need when you come: to be quiet or make noise; to be held firm or gently; to cry; to move or be still?

ANTICLIMAX

Did you have an orgasm? As importantly, did he or she? We usually know whether we have climaxed, but it is more difficult, particularly in a new and unfamiliar relationship, to tell when and whether our partner has done so. For him, it is difficult to know whether to carry on; for her, it can be hard to tell whether he is able to.

His signs of orgasm may seem all too obvious. In pleasuring by hand or mouth, the spurt of semen, thick and viscous, is a signal hard to ignore. It is sometimes useful to chart the signs just before this happens: the rush of blood up the penis, the minute spurt of pre-semen moisture, the sudden violent hardness felt in hand or mouth. These signs can prepare us for what is about to happen in whatever way is appropriate.

In penetrative sex, however, here may be some confusion. A feeling of tightness as the penis expands in the vagina, perhaps the pump of ejaculation itself, the increased moisture of the semen – all these may be clearly felt. Yet often, they may not. Calibrate instead his rising noise, the sudden increase in speed and thrust, the breathing changes and colour shifts. He will often grimace in a particular way, drawing his lips back or blowing out through his mouth. He may cling to his partner or bear down, suddenly want kissing or facial contact; he may reach for breasts or buttocks. He may simply breathe out and relax.

With her, it may not be so easy to calibrate correctly. Signals vary. Noise and violent movement may mean great arousal but not the climax itself; equally, she may come with a small sigh, or go quiet and pale. Easier to read are those signs that parallel his response: tightened muscles; a sudden increase in body contact; legs wrapped around; arms clutching.

With pleasuring by hand or mouth, the task of telling is easier. There may be a sudden rush of wetness or a sudden change in the texture of the body fluid. Taste or smell may subtly shift. The vagina can alter its angle or tightness, and a finger inside may be gripped by the contractions. With penetration there is more dependence on eye and ear, although vaginal movement is often there for the sensitive penis to respond to.

Her temptation, of course, may be to fake; easy to do because the signs of almost-orgasm can be so close to the signs of orgasm itself. Noise, movement, breathing patterns and heart-rate can be so bound up with that of a partner that it is impossible to separate them; and it is very easy, if he then has his climax, to let his passion take her signals over the edge too, and for her to fail to tell the truth afterwards.

So what, then, are the foolproof signs of her climax? Are there any ways of being sure? With a new lover, only vaginal contractions are truthful, though the delicate, rosy flush of orgasm across the chest is rarely seen without the real thing.

Most classic signs – rising noise, clutching hands, talking dirty – may as easily be a sign of loving complicity as of true climax. It takes time to learn a lover's orgasm patterns.

While a woman who does not orgasm may worry, a man who lacks an erection may panic. Equally, long periods spent without her achieving orgasm may undermine his confidence, for he may be convinced that her non-climax is his fault. The only genuine route to tackling any of these problems is by supporting and sharing the concerns of our partner. For in committed relationships, what creates problems is not the absence of love but the presence of fear: fear of failure; fear of disapproval; fear of disappointment. All these block orgasm, and the only way round this is honest communication.

If we suspect that a partner is faking, that she has not come or that he has lost his erection, we should address the fear first. We can cuddle,

reassure, offer body contact, use kisses and touch to communicate continued love. If it feels scary to talk, then we can ask obliquely if there is anything else our partner needs, or simply offer it and see if it creates a response. A partner's lack of orgasm is no crime, and if we keep close and stay communicating, then this state of affairs will not last for ever. The most positive thing is to return to asking and showing what arouses. When orgasm can be counted on, then the fear will disappear.

Sometimes he or she nearly climaxes when the love-making has to stop for some reason. In this situation, sensations will be strong for both partners. He may feel unbearable arousal in penis and testicles. She may still carry sensation in thighs, buttocks, genitals, breasts and belly. Both may turn this sexual tension into non-sexual tension; irritability or even anger. We can tell when this is happening by watching for high, shallow breaths, clenched stomach or back, voice tone rising or becoming short and sharp. We can tackle this tension in ourselves by conscious relaxation, deep breathing and shaking the energy from our limbs. We can offer our partner a brief massage of stomach, back or relevant comfort zone to take away the accumulated tension before it builds. Alternatively, not achieving climax can be an erotic delight, leaving us in a state of arousal all day, or at least until the next time we have a chance to be alone. We can revel in the sexual tension as we go about our daily work, and we can promise ourselves to come back to the uncompleted task at the next available opportunity and, this time, to take it all the way through to the end.

She shows many of the classic signs of arousal but is she coming? Perhaps in time she can develop sound and movement codes that tell him undeniably that she is near her climax, and then that she has reached it. Words, noises, a particular tension in her body or a clutch of her hands will reassure him.

AFTERWARDS

Arousal is over, at least for a while. But the time immediately afterwards may still be a vital part of love-making, for our bodies continue to communicate after passion has died. The messages we send then are just as vital as the ones we send in the heat of orgasm.

A first reaction, after our breathing has quietened and our heartbeat slowed, will often be to get comfortable, to ease away the muscle tension that has gone unnoticed as arousal dims all sense of pain. Notice the shifts that mark the untwining of bodies and the resettling into an easier and more supportive configuration. He may be acutely sensitive, unable to bear touch on his penis; she may want to hold her genitals in a comforting gesture.

After getting comfortable, there are two main kinds of reaction: a languorous sense of well-being that needs only to lie and dream; or an energized strength that wants to move and act. The former makes us feel totally relaxed and drained; thoughts are gone, worries have fled. From the outside, a partner may see flushed skin, closed or half-closed eyes, drooped face and limp limbs. Breathing is quiet, deep and slow. Skin feels warm and soft, muscles are relaxed and heart-rate has slowed. The voice may be slurred, soft and quiet, almost childlike.

Occasionally, such relaxation has an edge to it, a need for separateness and internal focus. But the need will usually be for holding and being held, for soft touching, for talking in quiet, confiding voices and gaining a feeling of gentle closeness. This may be the time to talk, to make

Left. They exchange words of love as their bodies come to rest after orgasm. His erection gradually dies away, his testicles move back down to their original position. Her uterus remains open for perhaps half an hour to allow sperm to travel upwards towards her ovaries, then returns, as does her whole vaginal area, to its normal size. Her breasts start to return to their normal sensitivity, the areola reduces and the nipples may flatten. For both partners muscle tone softens and breathing and heart-rate normalize. Their skin dries off the perspiration of arousal and returns to its everyday levels of sensitivity.

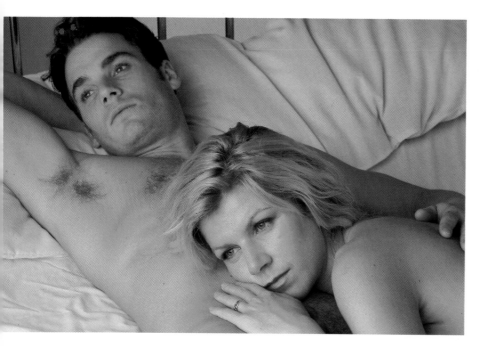

Left. A common pattern is for one partner to feel the need to disengage and be internally focussed, at least for a while. This is signalled by moving away physically, turning over or closing the eyes. If the other wants to be close, and sees this body talk as a rejection or a negation of the relationship, then real problems can arise. Being able to accept a need for emotional distance as natural after love-making requires trust and communication from both partners.

declarations of love or to share past experiences. It may be time to dream of the future. Or it may be the time to drift to sleep together.

Or maybe love-making will lead to the second kind of response, a lively energy that feels it can conquer the world. From inside, this makes us feel strong and active, perhaps even edgy; we want to move, to talk, to celebrate, to act. A partner may see us fidgeting, turning over, unable to lie still. Eyes will be open, muscle tone high, with tension still present as adrenalin takes time to drain away. Breathing is high and fast, the heart-rate back up to normal, the voice fast and energetic. Perhaps the words never stop. Here, the need is for movement: talking; getting food; taking a shower; getting up and going out. Perhaps we tease, play or pick a mock-fight; this mood is more likely than any to lead to the post-orgasmic row.

These are two extremes; there are many stages in between. Relaxation may turn to a need for action; an initial burst of energy may be followed by collapse into sleep. The problem is when responses do not match; when he is sleepy and she wants to eat, when she is relaxed and he wants to go out. Then both have to be willing to shift towards the other, paralleling each other's

EXPLORATION
Here are some considerations for the time immediately after love-making.
● What do you need in terms of: what you do; what you say; how you feel? What do you need from your partner? How can you tell what you need? How does what you need vary in different situations? How do you communicate your needs to your partner?
● What does your partner need in terms of: what he or she does, says and feels? What does your partner need from you? How can you tell what is needed? How does your partner communicate his or her needs to you?
● Where your needs differ, how can you communicate these and work out ways of meeting both your desires?

movement, voice tone, breathing and energy level until both come to match.

What next? We begin to wriggle and get uncomfortable, to lose our gentle bedroom voices and the soft, fluid movement that goes with arousal. These are signs that love-making is over, and it is time to move back to the world. Alternatively, after a while, we may turn to each other again. The stir of an erection may disturb her sleep; her hands may begin to explore him. Sensation returns; it is time to begin again.

Chapter Four
BUILDING ON LOVE

Once we have made love with our partner, all kinds of sexual and emotional possibilities are open to us. We may make the decision not to see that partner again; but if we do want to continue, then with every meeting, every touch and every act of sexual loving, we will build our relationship and its potential.

This chapter looks at the possibilities of a continuing sexual relationship in two dimensions, physical and emotional. The two are, in fact, dependent on each other, for our ability to feel physical sensation is linked to our ability to feel emotional sensation. So by learning new ways of giving, receiving and prolonging physical pleasure, we can increase the potential of our emotional relationship. And, by exploring and enhancing our emotions, we will increase the possibility that our sexual relationship will give us more and more delight.

The wide range of emotions we feel for each other within a sexual relationship may be challenging. We may find ourselves facing emotional dishonesty, lack of interest in sex or the trauma of the eternal triangle. Conversely, we may be challenged to develop our intimacy: bringing innovations into the bedroom; exploring fantasy; beginning to reveal our deepest emotions.

Once we face these challenges, with the help of our body-talk skills, we will then be able to turn them into positive experiences. In the end, if we are able to integrate our feelings and our desire, our reward will be a lifelong love built on truly firm foundations.

Once we have made a commitment to each other, then the emotions
of day-to-day living will become part of our relationship. Body talk can help us
cope. Here, her drooped, internally-focussed posture shows her grief; he lovingly
matches her position while keeping himself externally focussed in order to give
her attention. His arm around her is emotionally supportive, even though it
communicates his parallel drained emotional state in the way it hangs.

AN EMOTIONAL VOCABULARY

To read body talk accurately, we have to be emotionally fluent. When forming a loving relationship, we need to know the full range of emotions, to have what we might call an emotional vocabulary, and to be able to recognize such feelings in our partner. In our modern society this can be uncomfortable. We fight shy of feelings, push them down and discourage them. Yet if we suppress our feelings in everyday life, we will soon start to do the same in bed; and if we stop noticing, and reacting to, our partner's emotions, we may soon find that we have no one with whom to share our bed.

An emotional vocabulary is international; there is a surprisingly universal recognition of emotional signals. Japanese culture discourages the overt display of feelings, while Mediterranean cultures encourage it; nevertheless, the body talk of four of the five common emotions – happiness, anger, disgust, sadness – is clearly recognized world-wide. Only fear is often confused, in Western and Eastern cultures, with surprise.

When sad, we turn our focus inwards to mourn. We may feel unutterably heavy inside and, in reflection, our posture will droop downwards, our facial expression following, with mouth and eyes sunken or distant, our breathing slow and deep. Our voice will tremble as the tears overflow.

We will rarely know true terror, but throughout our life we may well be fearful or anxious from time to time. This will show in an inward, curled position as we unconsciously shield ourselves from real or imagined threats. Our colour will pale, our lips and hands tremble, as will our voice. A shaky stomach or a cold inner feeling will tell us that all our physical resources must concentrate on protecting us.

Confidence is the opposite of fear and is

Left. His inwardly directed signals spell fear or sadness. His eyes gaze into the distance, his face is pale, his lips set, his head turned away. Her reaction is stronger, closing her eyes as she retreats internally to cope with her rush of emotion, and reaching for him with her lips; the set of her face says that tears are not far away.

EXPLORATION
How do you know when you are feeling these emotions? How do you signal them to your partner? How do you show them externally? How does your partner show when he or she is feeling these emotions? Particularly, how do you know when your partner is in the early stages of feeling them?
• Anxiety; fear; confidence; surprise; irritation; anger; excitement; disgust; sadness; happiness.

Left. In grief, the first sign of tears is a gleam of moisture along the lower eyelid, with a reddening of the eyes, eyelids, cheeks and nose. The corners of her mouth are drawn downwards, as is the whole muscle tone of her face.

Right. A fearful gaze shows brows raised and drawn together and a slight frown on the forehead. Her eyes are open wide, the lower lid raised slightly and the mouth slightly open. If she was experiencing stronger fear, the lips would be drawn right back.

Above. A nervous expression also contains some anger. She reflects worry on her frowning forehead, but the curled lip indicates irritation. Her eyes glance sideways to spot the danger.

Above. A sideways glance and pursed lips show scepticism. The whole face is tilted to one side, the head turned at an angle to show that she believes something is not 'straight' here.

Above. This exaggerated pose mixes anxiety in the frown and uncertainty in the asymmetrical face. Her fingers to her mouth are reassuring, although they may also 'stop' her saying what she means.

shown in the reverse of all the above signals. An outward posture, straight and with head held high, is reflected in our direct gaze and even, steady breath. Our lips may smile slightly, our comfort zone feels relaxed and solid.

Anger is essentially an emotion of external focus, making us active in order to keep threats away. Adrenalin pumps through our body, arming us for action, giving us a sudden increase in movement and a rush of energy that can be felt deep in our stomach, back or chest. Our eyes open wide, as if to stare down an offender, our breath deepens. Our voice rises or hisses as if to scare off intruders.

Excitement uses many of the anger signals, but prepares us for positive action. The same rush of adrenalin keeps us moving, but this time our stomach tingles with excitement. Our wide eyes move, sparkling with moisture; our voice rises as we breathe high and fast to prepare ourselves for what is going to happen.

How can we use this basic emotional vocabulary? Whenever we feel the slightest sign of any of these emotions in ourselves or spot them in our partner, we have sensed a signal well ahead of time. We can then explore what is happening, encouraging positive emotions, and forestalling negative ones. And, through action, we can also aim to turn the negative signals into the relaxed, smiling, balanced, clear-eyed, steady-voiced signs of the final element in an emotional vocabulary – happiness.

HONEST BODY TALK

We all try to be honest, just as we all expect honesty from others. But is that expectation always practical? Emotions are often mixed, and people hardly know what they are feeling themselves. How can we spot mixed feelings: when passion is mixed with embarrassment; or apology is mixed with anger; when defensiveness is really based on fear; or agreement is actually a subtle refusal? Spotting emotional dishonesty and challenging it caringly, in ourselves and others, is the way to lay the foundations for a loving and honest relationship.

The first step is to spot mixed feelings in ourselves. These occur when we are saying one thing outwardly while feeling something else internally. If, for example, on the outside we are talking angrily, but on the inside we feel a shiver of fear; or if, on the outside, we say 'I love you' but on the inside we feel heavily sad; or if, on the outside, we nod, but on the inside our comfort zone churns in disagreement then, in all these cases, we are experiencing mixed feelings.

Other people's body signals also reveal when something is wrong. Look out for 'mismatches', where one signal comes from one emotion and another from elsewhere. A placating voice tone accompanied by an angry expression shows surface apology but hidden rage. A brilliant smile along with shaking hands shows surface confidence but inner tension. These signals can be almost unnoticeable micromovements of the emotion being hidden; they interrupt a facial expression momentarily and are gone again before we become aware of them.

Look out too for where 'pointers' contradict what we are saying: when expressions of concern are accompanied by body movements away from the object of that concern; or when denials of interest are accompanied by movements towards the person in question. In particular, look out for the false smile that, unlike its genuine counter-

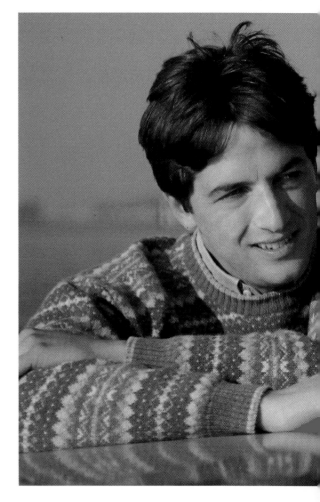

part, comes unspontaneously and at an inappropriate time in the conversation; it crosses our face too slowly, dies away spasmodically and is noticeably asymmetrical.

Be aware of any sign of body-talk tension: raised shoulders, tense back, minute halts in breathing or holding back our words in the way described on page 50. Finally, check for self-comfort signals: hand stroking face; arms hugging body and internal focus. What all these signals are saying is 'Help; I'm getting it wrong; please comfort me'.

How do we challenge mixed emotions? In

Above. She tries to smile with the bottom half of her face, but her staring eyes and raised shoulders reveal her true feelings: she is frightened, angry or a mixture of the two emotions.

ourselves, it demands awareness and the courage to admit when we do have more than one feeling to share, for it is fear that stops us being totally honest.

With a partner's mixed emotions, distance hinders. Move closer, making eye contact and touching supportively, before lovingly asking if he or she has anything more to tell you. The closer you are, the harder it will be for your partner to dissemble. Look for dropped eyes and signs of fear; these can indicate indecision about being honest. Be supportive as your partner begins to reveal real feelings.

Above left. They seem relaxed, with their crossed arms mirroring each other. But look more closely. His smile seems bright and externally focussed, but it mismatches his internal, defocussed gaze; his clenched fist could be a sign of tension. She looks into the distance, her shoulders hunched, her arms a barrier against contact. Her half smile may mask her feelings.

EXPLORATION
Consider these aspects of body-talk honesty.
● What are your inner signals signs of mixed emotions? How do you show them to your partner? What are your partner's inner signals of mixed emotions? How does he or she show them to you?

WHEN YOUR BODY SAYS NO

Everyone has their off-days. Everyone knows that sometimes, the erection does not come or the vagina does not moisten. Then, it is time to cuddle, and try again tomorrow. But what happens when tomorrow never comes, when every day is an off-day and sex is no longer on the agenda? What happens when for one or for both of us, our body simply says no?

In the deepest sense, this is body talk. Unless love-making has been impossible from the start, then our body did say yes originally. Now, with no interest and no desire, it is telling us that there is something wrong. We should listen.

There are many possible reasons why pleasure may have died. It could be a purely physical problem: we may be tired or ill; our hormone levels may have changed; or we may be taking medication (see Exploration). Alternatively, the reason could be that, now the first flush of passion is over, old memories are re-establishing themselves. Some past unhappy incident, sexual or emotional, may make sex distressing for us, or arousal something to be afraid of. This needs working through, and lack of desire is our body's way of encouraging us to do this. If so, we need the courage to talk it through and further courage, if necessary, to get counselling help. Sometimes, love is not enough; we also need professional friends.

Perhaps, though, it is not past trauma but current commitment that is the problem. It could be that our present relationship is beginning to bite, taking on emotional complexities that are tarnishing the lust we feel for each other. Love is still there, but the minor irritations are beginning to show, eroding at the trust or the commitment until sex has become a battleground. This too needs working through, but at home rather than away. Instead of being tempted to stray, we must keep (or start) talking to each other about what we think, what we feel, what we want. We need to use all our skills in body talk to communicate and understand each other anew. If the signals for leaving are there (see pages 106–107), then we will ultimately part. It is more likely, however, that we will keep going until we discover a new emotional connection. Then, with a shout of joy, our body will say yes again.

A final possibility is that, quite simply, too much sexual unfulfilment has passed under the bridge and, for one or both partners, sex is no longer worth the effort. If he has begun to lose his erection and this has spiralled into a panic every time she reaches for him, then his body will, quite sensibly, withdraw from the game. If she has failed to reach her orgasm, time after time, then her body may eventually decide that it is better not to feel any sensation at all.

In this case, go back to first principles. It is time to teach your body that there is another way, that sex does not have to be unfulfilling, and that it is time to try again. Agree between you that, for a while, perhaps a few weeks, you will not attempt to have intercourse at all. Then spend time each day just touching each other. Begin by touching only hands and head, moving on to feet, arms and legs the next day. Work through to intimate areas slowly, one day at a time. Touch a great deal. Hold an erogenous inventory (see pages 64–65). Talk, and develop your sexual codes once more.

When the time comes for penetration, hold back from orgasm for several days. At the start, simply penetrate, lying still for a while and really experience the feelings. Later, try moving just a little. Tell each other what your feelings are, but then withdraw and continue touching and arousing. Take several days to move to orgasm, and then only when both of you are absolutely ready.

If you take the time to teach your body that sex is something desirable, then ultimately your body will say yes to you again.

Above. He lies back while she takes charge. Perhaps he feels pressured to have his erection; by relieving him of the responsibility, she leaves him free to enjoy himself without worry.

Above. A reminder that, when regaining confidence in our ability to enjoy sex, timing is all-important. By synchronizing timing so that his climax (orange line) and her final orgasm (shaded area) occur together, both partners will be reassured.

EXPLORATION

Before deciding there are emotional or relationship reasons why your body is saying no, check none of these physical factors is affecting you.

- Are you chronically overworked, ill or have you recently had surgery?
- Are you greatly overweight?
- Have you recently suffered a traumatic event?
- Particularly for him: do you drink a lot? Are you on anti-depressants or drugs for high blood pressure?
- Particularly for her: are you on the Pill? Could it be the time of the month? Are you pregnant?

SEXUAL TRIANGLES

Is our relationship actually a sexual triangle? Is someone moving in to disturb the balance of our partnership? Is either of us responding to this? Triangular relationships – where one person is intimate with two others at the same time – are often understood only through body talk. Secrecy so often rules in affairs that it is only through non-verbal communication that we really appreciate what is happening.

Whether all three people know each other, or whether one person only is linked with the other two, body talk will alter as the triangle develops. The natural communication of intimacy between the original couple will change; new patterns of body talk will develop, both between the two new lovers and, if they ever meet, between the outsider and the other partner.

If you are an outsider moving in on an already existing partnership, you will use all the body language of early attraction that we have already seen. Preening, displaying, eye contact; all these will be there although, if under the watchful eye of a third party, they will be toned down – a touch under the table when no-one is looking or a brief, intimate smile in passing. If anything, you will be less friendly to your potential lover than you would be if you were simply friends. If you are the potential lover you will also be wary of showing too much, regardless of whether or not it was you who made the first move. You may be over-considerate to your partner, over-eager to be natural and unworried. But your mixed body talk will be obvious, your voice declaring no interest while your gestures point clearly at the new object of your desire.

If you sense an affair is possible but want to steer clear, then you have the choice to signal this with classic 'no' signs (*see* page 31): closed posture, turned-away movement, little eye contact. You could even try deliberate signals of mixed feelings, a false smile for example (*see*

Right. As three friends sit chatting, it becomes obvious what is going on under the surface. He sits closer to his partner, but his body and gaze are directed entirely towards the 'other woman'. He has eye contact with her and his hand movement is clearly directed towards her. Meanwhile, she is confident of her effect. She leans back in her chair, angled towards him and displaying with crossed legs and warm smile. Her posture is open, and she reaches out for him across the table, pushing her glass well into his intimate space. His partner is wary. She has moved very close to him, away from the other woman and well into his intimate space, while her hand on his wrist is a restraining rather than a comforting one. Although she looks towards the other woman, her gaze is a nervous, sideways one rather than the directly challenging stare of a woman who is confident about her relationship. Her mouth attempts a smile, but it is not a genuine one; her real feelings are anger and fear.

page 100), to put the outsider off completely.

If you are the existing partner, watching your lover contemplating an affair, check first whether there is any real danger. Even overt flirting may be part of your partner's response to flattery rather than a genuine attempt to have an affair. Check with whom he or she is matching body posture, verbal tone, breathing or directional pointers. If it is you, relax; if it is a potential lover, beware. Then consider what message you want to give to the outsider. You will rarely want them to succeed but, if you do, withdraw from your partner; show disinterest (not anger, which

This sequence shows how body language can determine the dynamic of a triangle and move a partnership from commitment into break-up. Interactions between all three parties create this outcome.

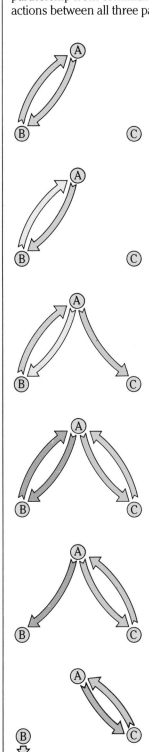

A and B have a relationship. They show their commitment to each other with affectionate body talk. C, meanwhile, is perhaps a friend or colleague of A. C meets A in another context completely, such as work.

For some unrelated reason, perhaps due to overwork, B begins to react to A by withdrawing or showing irritation. At first, A continues to show loving body talk, but eventually becomes frustrated.

A's frustration shows itself in angry signals to B, who becomes even more irritated than before. Increasingly, A starts to show interest in C who, flattered, responds with encouraging body talk.

Encouraged in turn by C, A's body-talk signals of interest increase, and this makes C more likely to respond positively. Meanwhile, A and B's non-verbal interaction becomes increasingly fraught.

While A and C continue to interact well, B, now confused by A's behaviour, withdraws completely, showing no affectionate body talk. A's anger increases; A turns increasingly to C for comfort.

Driven away by A's anger, B leaves. A meanwhile considers that B has been the culprit. C is the benefactor; by responding to A's interest, C has deeply affected B, though they have never met.

signals continued involvement); mismatch all your movements; lose eye contact; fail to listen when they talk. A potential intruder will be reassured and will move in closer. If you want the outsider to back off, be subtle; defensive antagonism may provoke a rise to the challenge. To be really subtle use all the body talk of real friendship: move close; smile warmly; match your movements; drop your voice to intimacy level; invite confidences and touch. In a curious way this will create enough of a bond between you to make it less likely that he or she will try to rock any boats.

SIGNS THAT IT'S OVER

How do we tell when a relationship is over? The signs of a partnership that has run its course are often very different from those of one that, though painful, is still alive. Even when body talk indicates constant irritation, when interactions erupt into daily rows and when break-ups are a regular part of life, involvement may still be there.

A relationship that is truly over, however, where one partner or the other has emotionally withdrawn, has none of these traumas; if it has, they are one-sided in the extreme. We can tell when we have reached this point if we feel almost no emotion at all. A sinking feeling in the stomach or a too-heavy relaxation in the muscles of the back, signal that our comfort zone now makes no response to the presence of this person. Other tell-tale signals may be a failure to smile even slightly at the thought of our partner or the sound of his or her voice; a lack of any sexual feeling when we are touched; and a lack of any strong emotional signals – even anger, fear or grief – when we interact. We no longer find our partner's body signals compelling; our breathing rates do not match any more, and his or her body smell and taste may seem wrong.

Right. The end is in sight, though neither of them may realize it. She is still involved, though angry, her direct gaze and flushed face showing her strong emotion. Her energetic hand movement shows the effort she is putting into making it work, though her other hand, nestling in her pocket, makes the gesture not entirely convincing. He, however, has withdrawn from the situation. Head down and body slumped, he reaches out to touch her, but the touch is placating rather than comforting. He simply wants her to stop being angry and let them get on with winding the relationship up. He has lost energy for it all and his movements betray this. In the end, it may be she who walks away, but it will be he who recovers his emotional equilibrium more quickly.

We may notice similar signs in a partner who has finally disengaged from us. If he or she prefers to keep an internal rather than external focus when we are together this signals that our company is no longer needed as much (though a need for some internal time is only natural, and no sign of a fading relationship). We will also notice that we have stopped matching each other with posture or gesture; we may only occasionally make or seek out eye contact; we will have stopped completing each other's sentences or picking up each other's voice tones. Our partner may seem respectful, but unresponsive; the voice will be low, unaroused and lacking energy. He or she will show little emotion, behaving in a calm and considered way.

This is not to suggest that neither of us will have strong feelings. Leaving a partner is not an unemotional act, even when there is no emotional involvement left. We may be anxious or fearful, with unease in our comfort zones, or cold hands or feet. We may feel angry or sad that the relationship has failed, and so feel the rush of adrenalin or be tearful and drained. But these are emotions about the past or the future; in the present, real emotional disengagement means that the person or relationship in question has no emotional – and therefore no physical – charge for us any more.

How can you tell, then, that it is really the end? One good way is to take some time to look at your own body talk when you consider ending the relationship; if you feel unable to chart your own reactions, get a friend to sit and talk things through with you, reporting on what is noticed. Try saying out loud a statement such as 'It is over'. Repeat it with all the signs of confidence: symmetrical posture; straight shoulders; erect head; front gaze and the minute, almost unnoticeable 'yes' nods that say that every part of you is in agreement. If, once you have done this, you

Above. Once the decision has been taken, half the pain often goes, and is is easier to offer each other support and comfort for the final stages of the relationship.

exhale deeply and feel calm, then this means the time is right to end the relationship. You may not feel deliriously happy, but your body and emotions, if not your mind, have made the decision for you. If you hear your partner talking about ending the relationship while showing the body talk described above, then it is time to accept the inevitable.

We often mistake our signals, however, thinking that our relationship is over when, in fact, we have simply reached a crisis point. If your response to the above statement is to feel strong emotion – tears of regret around your eyes, anger churning your stomach, an asymmetrical movement of your body, a slight shake of your head – then you are still emotionally involved. Whether you stay or go is your choice, but the emotional link may be worth fighting for.

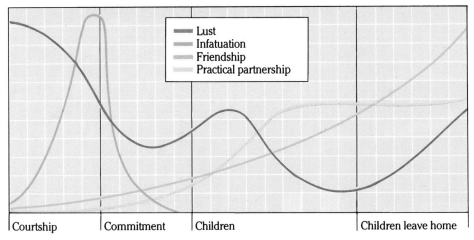

Lust
Infatuation
Friendship
Practical partnership

Courtship | Commitment | Children | Children leave home

Above. She gazes into the distance, obviously thinking of her lover. Is she in lust, where all her thoughts and feelings are concentrated on desire; or is she infatuated, where the uniqueness of her lover makes her addicted to him?

Left. Lust dips soon after love-making, while infatuation peaks and then falls swiftly. Practical partnership rises with commitment, levels off once children are gone, while friendship rises throughout a lifelong relationship.

ARE YOU IN LOVE?

We have met, we have been attracted, we have spent time together. We have kissed and touched. We have, at last and wonderfully, made love. We want things to continue, maybe for a long time.

But are we in love? Is this one, particular sexual relationship a special one? Is it a relationship that will mean total involvement, physical, mental and emotional? What will happen as things develop, as we get closer, as we become part of each other's lives? And how can body talk tell us what is happening?

At the start, most relationships with a high sexual component are based on what we might call lust. A first, visual contact will create strong physical desire that will in turn dramatically affect our body talk. Even before, perhaps especially before, we touch the object of our desire, we will imagine making love, and our body will respond. We may have almost constant erection and moistness, and awareness of our lips, skin, fingers and genitals. Others will notice us moving in a seeming haze, though most of what we feel will not be apparent.

When we do make contact, and usually after we have made love, two things happen. The high lust diminishes. Particularly for him, desire drops dramatically as soon as the first love-making session happens. After that, emotion may build, or desire for that one particular person may grow, but the constant desire fades away. At this point, many relationships fail. Seeking more stimulation, he or she may move to another conquest. Alternatively, they may settle to a routine sexual relationship with no emotional component. They may, however, move to infatuation. This next step in the process involves awareness of far more than physical desire, but includes similarly dramatic physical changes. We lose our appetite, lose sleep and lose weight. We love deep eye contact, our

heartbeat becomes irregular, our blood pressure rises. Others will notice us as restless, absent-minded, focussed entirely on our partner. Recent research suggests this comes from a chemical released in the brain, the 'love drug' phenylethylamine which has the same effect on the brain as a powerfully addictive substance.

In the long-term, however, phenylethylamine will wear off and our first infatuation will die. In body-talk terms, we feel less stimulated, emotionally and sexually. We will start sleeping regularly again, need less body and eye contact with our lover and start paying attention to other parts of our life. We calm, as both our high sexual drive and addiction diminish, while preparing ourselves for further commitment. The same research that highlighted phenylethylamine also suggests that this stage of a relationship is supported by a flow of other chemicals, enkephalins, that increase our capacity for disregarding difficulties and lessen our experience of pain. With this as a basis, we can embark on a practical and more demanding partnership, having common goals, working together, setting up home, bearing children.

A final, overlapping stage is creating a friendship with our partner. Separate from the practical aspects of commitment, it involves mutual approval and attention, with mental and emotional as well as sexual contact. We enjoy spending time with our lover, having mutual interests and sharing thoughts, feelings and experiences. The chemicals linked with this are endorphins, and the feelings of intense pleasure they give us make contented partnership possible. We may feel this in our comfort zone, or around our heart, maybe as an all-body feeling or simply an awareness of warmth and comfort. It will show in our body talk as an increasing ability to complement and match our partner's movements, as if we were one person.

TOUCH OUTSIDE THE BEDROOM

Of course we touch each other inside the bedroom, but what about outside it? As lovers, do we think that public touching is a taboo or an essential, a sign of intimacy or a sign of insecurity?

Touching outside the bedroom comes in many forms, from the social kiss on greeting through to surreptitious outdoor intercourse. But why do we do it? Perhaps it is sheer lust that eggs us on, particularly at the start of a relationship. Bed is just not enough; we need to continue touching, kissing and fondling, to keep at bay the intense arousal that drives us on. If we have no privacy in which to be sexual – as very young people lack in our society – perhaps the disco or the park is the only place to go. In the unbeatable privacy of several thousand people, we can hide our sexuality by flaunting it.

Or perhaps our reason for touching in public, particularly at the start of a relationship, is to show others what is happening. Stroking his cheek shows clearly that we are a couple. An arm round her waist states, 'Look, she loves me'. Such touches not only display our love to others, they also shout it to the world. We use large, noticeable gestures and movements: swinging arms, huge hugs, deep eye contact clearly visible from many yards away. It is more likely, however, that we will touch in public simply to reaffirm our relationship. Such touches are rarely overtly sexual, sometimes only slightly more intimate than contact between two friends. A kiss on meeting to re-establish contact after days or hours apart; holding hands while walking to add the vital element of touch to all our other communications; a snatched closed-mouth kiss in delight at what he has said; a tender stroking of hair in appreciation of what she has just done: all these are vital signs of our commitment as we move through the world together. The fact that these happen in the supermarket rather than the bedroom is the last thing on our mind.

Everyone has an opinion about touching: when; where; who and how. He may want to hug all the time; she may be more circumspect. She may feel blatantly sexual; he may just want to keep walking. Our personal preferences will rest on our background and the context of each situation. Perhaps past messages, from parents or teachers, have told us that public touch is unacceptable or, alternatively, that it is an essential sign of love. Perhaps gender stereotypes tell us that real men touch a lot, or that real women do not allow touching. Culturally too, we will differ: recent research on touch between acquaintances in various countries estimated 180 touches per hour in Puerto Rico, 110 in France, 2 in America and none at all in England. Even holding hands, seen as innocuous in most Christian countries, would be viewed as shameful in many Islamic ones.

But whatever our baseline ideas, each individual context will dictate acceptability. We might walk up to the office gates intertwined with a lover, yet not touch each other at all during the working day. We might be quite happy to kiss passionately in the back row of the movies, but would die of embarrassment if we discovered that two close friends were sitting in the row in front! Equally, our own personal-distance gauge tells us how near or how far we can let others approach us; and if they come close in the wrong context, we feel invaded and threatened, even if, that evening in bed, we let them approach very close indeed.

What happens, then, if our personal preferences mismatch, if one of us wants to touch and the other fights shy? We can tell our own misgivings if, when in public, we are more aware of other people's gaze than of our partner's desire to touch. We can tell our partner's misgivings if he or she shrinks away as we reach

A perfect match in their need for touch outside the bedroom. She takes the lead in kissing him intimately and publicly; her posture, leaning down over him and circling him with her arms, shows that, for this kiss, she is in charge. He is totally at ease. His tilted-back head is responsive and eager, while the fact that he does not reach up for her shows that, for the moment, he likes the passive role and the flattery of being kissed. Neither of them is checking what others think; their angled heads and closed eyes show awareness only of each other. This kiss is not for display, but for personal, intimate contact.

out, responding to touch with tense, tight, guarded gestures, keeping us at a distance with bulky parcels or carrier bags. Such preferences may cause distress. The toucher may well see withdrawal as a statement about lack of commitment or acceptance; the non-toucher may well feel embarrassed, trapped or invaded. Such divisions can cause eventual break-up, as we both fail to get our needs met at the deepest level. Better by far is when both of us agree on what level of touch we like, and on when, how and exactly how much we enjoy touching, both inside and outside the bedroom.

EXPLORATION
Look at the following list of contexts in which you and your partner might touch. Then look at the list of possible touches. Consider how happy you and your partner would be in each context with each touch.
● Context
In bed; in another room; in public place not overlooked; in crowded public place; in front of friends; at work.
● Touches
Holding hands; arm round waist; hands down back pocket of jeans; hugging; kissing on cheek; kissing with closed mouth; kissing with tongue; touching breasts; touching genitals; having intercourse.

CREATIVE ROWING

Many couples never row. Natural non-rowers, they move through their relationship in peace and contentment. But if you do row, then that is natural for your relationship, and you can learn from sexual body talk to use your rowing style creatively.

Rows are like love-making. They follow the same pattern, they call on many of the same physical processes and they are equal explosions of physical energy. Like sex, they can be handled mutually and with commitment to give physical release and emotional contact.

Both sex and rows begin slowly, with tiny cues. A feeling of biting back the words, a tense jaw or comfort zone, a rush of energy; all these are the foreplay of anger. Both passion and anger flood our body with adrenalin, and raise our heart-rate, blood pressure and breathing rate, preparing us for action.

Inhibiting anger guiltily, or letting one partner shout while the other placates, is as bad as non-orgasmic sex or a premature ejaculation. Adrenalin continues to race round the body, causing stress and tension, playing unknown havoc with the system. Better by far to do what we do in sex: move on to a climax. It will take effort from both of you, but once over the irritation threshold when you feel the rush of anger fill you, then together you can make it happen. Heighten your body talk as you would on the way to orgasm: raise your voices; speed up your breathing; strengthen your gestures. Steer clear of violence, as you would in sex. Always move together, as you would in sex. Do not be scared of what you will say; it will be no worse than any other row, and it will be over much more quickly. If both of you keep going with energy, you will find that the climax happens. You tip over into laughter, tears or sheer euphoria. Then you can hug and relax, in a post-orgasmic haze.

Below. Rows and orgasms take the same shape. Arousal or irritation (1 and 2) builds slowly but inexorably. The 'making love' diagram shows how orgasm (3), a physical 'explosion', floods the body with energy and brings release and relaxation (4). The 'rowing' diagram shows that, when rising anger is released by an emotional explosion (3) within the context of a loving relationship, then emotional energy floods in, bringing both physical and mental release and a reconciliation (4).

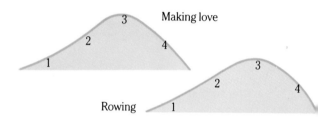

Making love

Rowing

Below. Just as an early orgasm can bring a premature end to love-making, leaving the other partner unfulfilled (left-hand diagram), so an imbalanced anger explosion within a relationship is unsatisfactory, leaving one partner guilty and the other resentful. Equally, (right-hand diagram) just as love-making with no release whatsoever leaves both partners on the edge of orgasm, so inhibiting anger within a relationship leaves simmering irritation that totally drains all energy.

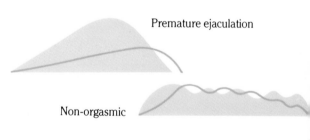

Premature ejaculation

Non-orgasmic

EXPLORATION
How do you know when you are preparing to have a row with your partner? Recall the very first signs that tell you a row is on its way.
● You
What internal sensations do you have? How does your comfort zone feel? Is there any particular part of your body that signals to you that trouble is coming?
● Your partner
What posture does he or she take? What do you notice about eyes, mouth, facial expression/tension? Does skin colour, warmth or moisture change? How does the voice sound?

Left. They start from a point of unspecified emotion. Their staring eyes, pale faces and tension on back and neck muscles are ambiguous body-talk signals. His hands on her arms could be aroused or violent; her fist on his chest could be forceful or passionate. Perhaps they are angry, or perhaps they are aroused. Which is it?

Above top. They move closer together, his hands tightening on her arm, while her hands are moving up towards his neck. The situation has, even at this stage, lost its ambiguity as we can already see the signs of passion emerging. She meets his gaze and it is evident that the sexual energy has started to flow between them.
Above bottom. The direction of this interaction is becoming even more clear. The tension between them brings them yet closer together, with passionate emotional contact. At any moment they will move into an embrace. It is now obvious that the starting point of ambiguous emotion has transmuted into real passion.

Above. They move closer together, his hands beginning to tighten on her arm, while her hands are gradually moving up towards his neck. Already we can see the signs of passionate anger emerging from both partners. She meets his gaze and it is evident that the angry energy has started to flow between them.

Above. The direction of this interaction is becoming even more clear. The tension between them brings them yet closer together with furious emotional contact. At any moment, they will fully erupt. It is now obvious that the starting point of ambiguous emotion has turned into full-blown anger.

SEXUAL HEALING

Love-making inevitably raises strong feelings. If done well, it arouses every part of our body to heights of sensation we have rarely experienced before. But love-making raises strong feelings in other ways too, and these can often spiral out of control. So where we find passion, we may also find passionate disagreement, and where we find orgasm, we may also find tears.

As we have seen, our emotions communicate with us through body talk; we may feel excitement in the pit of our stomach, and anger as a tight band across our chest. Then, when we make love, and all our body sensations are heightened, our emotions have an increased opportunity to make their presence felt. As if some channel of communication has been opened more fully, we feel more during sex, and some of this is strong emotion.

When we make love, we also fall in love to some extent. We have someone with whom we can trust our emotions, both positive and negative. We may need to talk through our feelings of insecurity about past lovers, we may want to share our current irritations, we may want to reveal our hopes and fears about the future. Emotional issues that we would never talk through with a colleague are ripe for discussion with a partner, and love-making may be the ripest time.

As we start to become aroused, so our emotions rise. As we move towards orgasm, so our joy, fear, anger or grief may, almost unnoticed, come to the surface. As we climax – or before or after climaxing – then comes the euphoria, the anger or the fear. Our emotions follow our physical reactions up the scale of feelings until they peak inexorably and have to be expressed.

It could be that we do this alone, with our own emotions feeding off themselves. Or it could be that each of us urges the other on to stronger feeling, as we do in love-making, just by our reactions. It could be that, rather than crying alone, we row together; just at the point when we feel we should be closest, we seem to be attacking each other with emotion.

How can we tell when our emotions are thus triggered? With fear, she may find herself resenting the invasion of penetration, while he may be worried that the erection will not happen. During intercourse, anger may make him thrust violently, or desperately; when pleasuring him, anger may make her movements hard and uncontrolled, or slow and resentful.

Grief may make us internally focussed, heavy and passive in love-making, while embarrassment will cast a damper over everything, with breasts hidden, legs opened only for intercourse, eyes averted, and voices muted. Joy, or spiralling euphoria, may send both partners into spasms of hysterical delight; though it is not unusual for this later to tip over into post-coital *tristesse* (sadness as the French call it.

All this is, in fact, positive. Revealing our emotions in this way can be an instant route to developing our friendship. For if, in the loving context of our partner's bed, we can begin to explore and express our emotions, then we will enhance our relationship immediately. Even if our strong emotions lead us to attack each other, we need to accept that this is largely in the nature

Right. This diagram is a broad representation of how, in orgasm, emotions as well as sensations can spiral into a waterfall of feeling. When we are physically aroused, our body sensations rise inexorably to a peak until they have to tip over the edge. Similarly, feelings can rise and rise during arousal, feeding off each partner's emotional energy until they can have no resolution but an orgasm-like crescendo. It is no coincidence that when passions rise, so do our emotions.

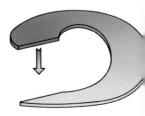

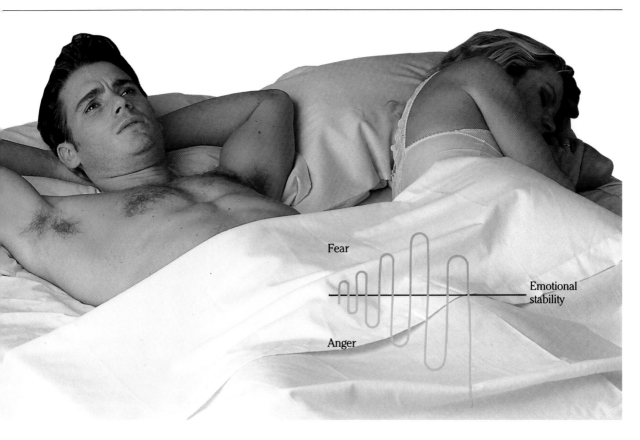

Fear

Emotional
stability

Anger

Above. Love-making has created an emotional explosion. Now, however, instead of welcoming the opportunity to explore it, they have seen it as a problem and turned away. His furrowed brow and open-arm position show he is thinking it through; her bowed shoulders and curled posture show she is comforting herself. Together, they could be talking it out and resolving the issue.

Above diagram. A typical pattern of emotional crisis. While making love, one partner becomes mildly irritated with the other. This then slips into fear of disturbing the progress of arousal, but then turns into resentment that a partner has noticed nothing wrong. Fuelled by the physical sensations of love-making, emotion spirals and tips over into a full-blown waterfall.

of our love-making. Just as our strong physical sensations are caused by contact with each other, so our strong emotional energy is a result of our emotional contact. So be prepared, just occasionally, to use sex as a form of emotional healing. If an outburst happens, reassure yourselves firstly that most distress comes from the past and is probably no critical reflection on your current relationship. Perhaps think back to the past, and allow yourselves to recall any memories that may be linked with the feeling, you have shown, whether they be happy or sad.

Then take the time to talk through what you experience, what you feel, what you remember: find out why she felt great sorrow during arousal; or why he was suddenly afraid after orgasm. Share tears or anger about her past abortion. Talk about the previous partner who laughed at his technique. Allow yourselves to resolve your feeling about the past.

And, if courage is really high, try returning to the very point where emotion rose, and begin again. Make love again until the feeling rises, and then allow the tears to come, the anger to explode, the fear to shake, but this time with both of you prepared. When faced fairly and squarely and linked with the powerful sensations of love-making, positive feelings can be enhanced by sex and negative feelings can transmute. Grief and fear can die away for ever in the safety of a partner's arms. Embarrassment can slink out, never to return. And anger can transform itself into a howling, screaming, best-ever orgasm.

115

INNOVATIONS

Good sex keeps on changing. While a dying relationship, or one in which our body is saying no to sex (*see* pages 106–107 and 102–103 respectively), will benefit only in the short term from sexual innovations, a relationship that is stable and happy gains added spice from the introduction of something new.

The first step is to notice where things need changing. A sigh of pleasure when we move into a favourite position in sex means that this should be kept in the repertoire; a slightly different sigh may mean that the repertoire needs expanding. A particular way of pleasuring your partner may work every time; but if it makes you tense then make a change.

Sometimes our sexual needs alter over time, but we have neither realized it yet, nor truly communicated it to our partner. Perhaps we now want oral sex when we fought shy of it before. We may find ourselves pushing upwards if our partner kisses our stomach, or offering oral sex ourselves in the hope that it will be reciprocated. If something that once drove us wild now creates discomfort, we may flinch, willing our partner to take the hint. There is nothing to stop us requesting these changes openly; and nothing to stop a partner being just as honest. But when a relationship is sound and stable, maybe we are reticent because we do not want to spoil things, or to rock the boat.

Body talk can make the introduction of sexual variations non-threatening. Begin by thinking of ways to signal innovations to your partner more clearly. Often, all that is needed for understanding is a stronger signal. Make sure that, as you start, you are feeling loving and not confrontational, or your partner will, quite rightly, get defensive. Then, once relaxed, emphasize the positive signs you are giving and play down the negative ones. If your aim is to experiment with a new position, wait until you are both aroused, then signal your pleasure clearly as you move to the new configuration. No lover will be able to resist you if your enthusiasm is high. If your need is for your partner to stop doing something that you do not enjoy, then let your pleasure signal die away during this activity; then, as your partner moves on to something more comfortable for you, show clearly, by noise and movement how much better this is.

In a loving partnership, there is the temptation to say yes constantly. We know she likes to do it this way, so every time, however wrong it feels, we feed back moans of delight. Why not? This is a partnership. But if something else would be nicer after a while, we should love each other enough to let our body talk be honest.

And perhaps, we sometimes need to verbalize what we want in order to communicate it to our partner: asking for safe sex; suggesting love without intercourse. But it can be all too easy in this situation to let our body talk undermine the words we speak. Our words say, 'Here's something fun we could do'; but our nervous smile or defensive eyes say, 'I'm scared of asking this' or 'I'll be angry if you don't say yes'. Our partner thinks, 'Perhaps it isn't all that much fun after all'. Then we wonder why he or she says no.

Uncertain emotions (*see* pages 100–101) will sabotage the best innovations from the start. Do not over-smile, bite your lip or use nervous gestures; your partner will pick up on your uncertainty and use it to fuel his or her own. Instead, show your love, concern and above all enthusiasm for what you are suggesting. Choose a time when you are both enjoying each other's company, and maybe aroused. Make direct eye contact, breathe evenly and relax. Remind yourself that your aim is to create more pleasure, and a better relationship. You therefore have a right to ask for innovations. Explain what you want and why it would be wonderful.

Above. If a partner does respond badly to a suggestion, then our support may be needed. She is keeping him at a distance with her crossed arms; her tilted head and downcast eyes indicate that she is feeling strong negative emotion. His answer is to move in close but not too close, one hand on her back, perhaps supporting a comfort zone. He also keeps looking at her, showing her by his attention that he will take the time to listen and talk things through. But he is neither apologizing nor getting angry at her response, neither backing down nor demanding that she agrees. He has made his suggestion and now waits to work things though.

Above. She has something to suggest, but is afraid to do so. Her attempt to placate is clear from the false and asymmetrical smile and the raised eyebrows and lower lids. She is not too sure about what she is proposing, and the chances are that he will never be either.

Left. A confident and genuine smile, reflected in her clear and direct gaze, shows the love with which she makes her suggestions. Her expression is balanced, her smile symmetrical, her stance direct; she evidently knows what she wants. What partner could resist whatever innovation she is suggesting?

EXPLORATION

Look at this list of possible innovations. How easy or difficult would you find signalling each one to your partner? How do you think your partner would respond to each one you suggested? Would you feel hurt or threatened by any of them, if suggested to you by your partner?

- Asking my partner to do something different
- Asking my partner to stop doing something he or she likes doing
- Telling my partner I do not want to make love
- Telling my partner that something he or she does is uncomfortable for me
- Asking my partner to delay penetration
- Asking my partner to delay orgasm
- Asking my partner to speed up his or her orgasm
- Saying I want to make love without intercourse
- Saying I want to have intercourse without foreplay
- Suggesting sex for quick release rather than intimacy
- Suggesting oral sex
- Suggesting a new position
- Suggesting making love in a new place
- Showing/asking what is liked in masturbation
- Showing/asking exactly what is liked in intercourse
- Suggesting we use a sex aid
- Suggesting reading sexy magazines or books
- Suggesting using safer sex methods
- Suggesting using contraception

WHAT PART ARE YOU PLAYING?

We all have different sides to our personality. At work we are one person, with friends we are another. In bed, we have the chance to let whole parts of our personality come through. These are not fantasy roles, but sides of us that may or may not come out in normal life. Perhaps we are usually a gentle person, but in the safety of our lover's arms, we can tumble violently round the bed to our heart's content. Rough, tough, meek, mild, gentle, passionate, calm, excited: we can give vent to any side of us we wish, and leave it in bed as we go about our day-to-day routine.

Perhaps we may want to return to our childhood. Men may find it particularly difficult to be helpless and passive, but it may also be something for which they yearn. Watch for a partner signalling a need to be babied by curling up small; or talking in a babyish way with softened or lisped syllables. In response to this, try taking all his or her weight on your knees or chest, surrounding your partner completely with warm legs or nestling him or her in the crook of an arm. He may also like to nuzzle a breast, but in a very different way from when aroused.

Complementary to the child is the parent. We may take on a caring role, looking after the other person in practical ways, offering food and drink, leaning over and stroking or cuddling up. With gentle voice, we may signal that we are giving love. A good response to a partner who wants to play parent is to lie back and relax, letting yourself be cared for as long as it feels right.

Being helpless or in charge is another pair of complementary sides to personality. We may signal a need to be helpless by starting a mock fight and then giving in, by reaching arms above head during intercourse so that the other will pin us down, or by any stretched-out movement that leaves our centre unguarded. When playing the 'in-charge' part, we may fulfil the needs of a

helpless partner or initiate our own game by starting a fight in order to win, speaking roughly or giving orders, or taking charge during intercourse. When the roles of being helpless and in charge play together, the latter may bring the former almost to the point of orgasm, sometimes keeping a partner there for delicious hours.

A word about gender roles here. If she is allowing her helpless part to come out, she may feel guilty about enjoying being dominated; he may feel equally guilty about wanting to be in charge. But in this loving situation, both can allow these parts of themselves to come out,

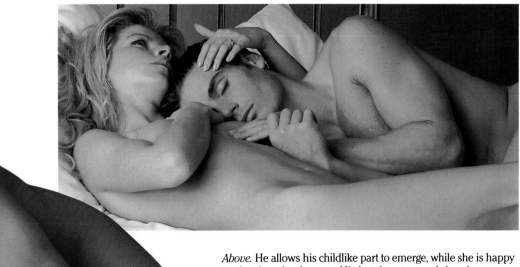

Above. He allows his childlike part to emerge, while she is happy to play the role of parent. His foetal posture and closed eyes reveal how deeply he needs to be nurtured; she strokes his brow, while 'watching over' him in a typical parent position.

Left. She plays helpless, while he is in charge. Her smile shows that she is enjoying herself, while he is pretending to be masterful and finding it quite amusing. In a moment, he will begin to arouse her, and the mood will change again.

> EXPLORATION
> Consider your role-playing during love-making.
> ● Which of these sides of your personality are you aware of: baby; parent; helpless; in charge; clown? How do you express this part of your personality in love-making? How would you like to express this part of your personality in love-making? How could your partner help you to do this? Would you feel threatened if your partner revealed any of these personality roles in bed?

knowing that in fact it is she who is in complete control; one genuine protest from her and he would abandon his role at once.

When we let our clown side run riot, we love having fun in bed. We will signal clown mood by lots of smiles and laughter. We will often like physical horseplay, making mock forays to our own or a partner's genitals, not to be in charge or to arouse, but to tease. The clown likes to experiment, try things out, use cream in aerosol cans or silly sex toys. Our clown personality is fun to have around; respond to it light-heartedly, with lots of matching laughter and horseplay,

and absolutely no disapproval at all.

Finally, we may give rein to our rebel part when we are feeling outrageous. We may innovate, introducing new things, suggesting new positions, using dirty language. A rebel will wait for others to be shocked, and sulk slightly if they are not, perhaps letting mock anger show or hitting a few pillows; though rarely with deep feeling, more often in a playful mood. Rebel behaviour often lasts for only a few minutes or hours, but allows us really to let go of our inhibitions. And, because of that, perhaps all lovers should play the rebel sometimes!

FANTASIES

We all like to dream, and often our dreams are of a highly sexual, erotic nature. In the safe context of the bedroom, we can often make these dreams come true by acting out our sexual fantasies with a willing, understanding partner.

But how can we communicate our fantasies in a safe way; and how can we tell what our partner's fantasies are? Often we are blocked by

Using props and added extras can enhance any fantasy. Our body often responds to the feel of shiny materials such as rubber o leather; they may call up memories, or bring to mind authority o rebel figures whom we admire and who arouse us. They are ofter tied in with dominance or submission fantasies.

ear; our dreams may include violence, acted out or suffered; they may seem unethical or even immoral; they may be so wild that we could never imagine doing them; so how can we admit them, let alone act them out?

It is wise to trust our instincts; this very wariness is our protection. Obviously some fantasies – the illegal, the dangerous, the violent – should not be transferred into reality. But in

most cases, our fantasies are literally the part of us that we are happy to keep in our heads, separate from everyday life. The people who truly accept their own fantasy life are never in danger of making it real.

We can subtly move our partnership into fantasy mode by noting what our partner responds to. Look out for the first signs of a preference or response: a gleam of interest if looking through a book; a second glance at a magazine; the classic signs of arousal (pupil dilation, skin-colour change, parted lips, sexual tension) when watching a video. Notice your partner reaching out to touch you when such stimuli are around, and give an equally strong response if these things are what turn you on too.

Make the most of arousing fantasies. When faced with a book about voyeurism or a film about a *ménage à trois*, use the desire generated to bring you together. Do not feel guilty if the visions in your head are of sex with a stranger, while the person in your arms is a regular partner. Unless fantasy is the only way you can ever get aroused, what you are doing is quite natural: using thoughts to fuel your pleasure in each other's touch.

Then, move to talking. When very aroused, try whispering snatches of your fantasies, or asking eagerly for hints of those of your lover. Stop immediately if you sense any distaste – a pull-back or a turn away – and then probably decide never to explore that particular element of a fantasy again. But if talking hastens your arousal, and you both respond with desire, then move perhaps to a hint of reality. Strip slowly and erotically when you next undress, pin her hands above her head next time you make love, talk dirty next time you masturbate him. Play, experiment, exaggerate, amuse. Body talk need not be real to arouse; the body talk of fantasy can be even more effective than that of real life.

EXPLORATION

Which of these fantasies have you had and enjoyed?
● Sex with a past partner; sex with a stranger; sex with two or more people; orgies; sado-masochistic; being forced; watching or being watched; exposing yourself; sex with a famous person; striptease; sex with someone much younger or older; bisexuality; being a prostitute; doctors and nurses; being made love to by someone in authority.
What body signals do you give when you fantasize? How do you act out these fantasies in bed? How could your partner help you to do this? How could you tell your partner about a previously unshared fantasy? Which of these fantasies would you find arousing if your partner shared them in bed?

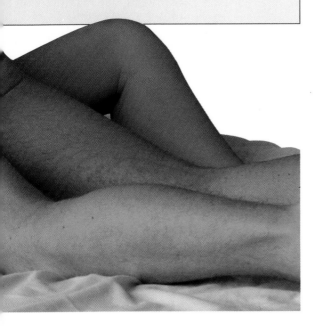

LIFELONG LOVE

What exactly is lifelong love? When we have moved through the stages of first attraction, first lust and first love; when we have explored each other's bodies and each other's minds; when we have made our sexual commitment and our emotional promise; when we have coped with problems and worked through conflict: what do we find at the end?

A couple committed to a lasting relationship will move, over time, to a deep understanding of their mutual body talk. They may not always be aware of it as the best body talk is unconscious, intuitively happening when it needs to happen, with no worry or effort. But a couple with lifelong love will, whether they know it or not, share the same body-talk vocabulary, and give and receive complementary body-talk messages. They often move in the same way, taking up similar postures and using similar gestures even when apart. They have borrowed each other's movement patterns, each other's speech patterns, accents and voice tones. Often, they use each other's key phrases, echoing each other with every word they speak.

Often, lifelong lovers even develop the same physical weaknesses over time, matching each other on the level of illness or disease. Such couples tend to keep close, but are intuitively aware of each other's distance-comfort zones, moving close but not too close, respecting each other's physical privacy even when they have lived together for forty years. They often have similar ideas about touching in public, for if these had differed, maybe the strain on their relationship would have proved too much.

Such a couple will still preen, display and flirt with each other, but in the safety of knowing that they are committed to each other; they show off for each other's benefit, rather than to catch or trap. Though they may do so unconsciously, they often block each other off from other people when in company, seeking each other's attention first, spontaneously using patterns of movement and speech that effectively leave others excluded.

They can often predict each other's behaviour just from the body talk; they can tell a partner's mood from the slam of the door, or can move forward to offer assistance when no one else has spotted the need.

Lifelong couples have lifelong sex with each other. Each partner knows just what the other likes, and they have developed a sophisticated code that tells them just what is needed in bed. They know what positions, movements, speeds and rhythms suit. Sometimes they may take turns to get fulfilment, but are able to climax mutually when they choose to. They are securely flexible about their needs in bed because they know that, in the long run, these needs will be met. And they sense when change is needed because they know each other's signs so well, and work to accommodate most, if not all, needs.

Lifelong couples have a good time in bed because they are emotionally knowledgeable about each other. They have learned over time to read each other's emotions at a deep level, and to allow time and space for those emotions to be felt. They know when one or the other is distressed, and so are able to offer support; they know when one or the other is euphoric and are able to join in. They have many problems, just the same as other people, but they use their emotional and body-talk knowledge to work through worries, problems, and crises, in bed as well as out of it.

In the end, though, if we are a lifelong couple, we may well not need to talk much – about our feelings, our sexuality, our past or our future – because we only have to look, listen and feel to understand each other's body talk. And we have learned to turn that body-talk understanding, day by day, into lifelong love.

RESOURCES

Further Reading

Bandler, Richard and Grinder, John. *Frogs into Princes*, Mowab Utah, Real People Press, 1989

Bateson, Gregory. *Mind and Nature*, London, Fontana, New York, E.P. Dutton, 1980

Bateson, Gregory. *Steps to an Ecology of Mind*, New York, Ballantine Books, 1972

Berne, Eric. *Games People Play*, Harmondsworth, Penguin, 1968

Cameron-Bandler, Leslie. *Solutions*, San Rafael California, Future Pace, 1985

Comfort, Alex (ed.). *The Joy of Sex*, London, Quartet, 1972

Darnborough, Ann and Kinrade, Derek. *The Sex Directory*, Cambridge, Woodhead Faulkner, 1988

Gunn, S.L. *The Challenge of Excellence*, Lake Oswego Oregon, Metamorphous Press, 1986

Hall, Edward T. *The Silent Language*, New York, Doubleday & Co., 1959

Hite, Shere. *The Hite Report*, London, Unwin Paperbacks, 1976

Hite, Shere. *The Hite Report on Male Sexuality*, London, Macdonald Optima, New York, Alfred A. Knopf Inc., 1978

Hoffman, Lynn. *Foundations of Family Therapy*, New York, Basic Books, 1981

Kitzinger, Sheila. *Woman's Experience of Sex*, Harmondsworth, Penguin Books, 1983

Knapp, M.L. *Nonverbal Communication in Human Interaction*, New York, Rinehart and Winston, 1978

Lewis, Byron and Pucelink, Frank. *Magic Demystified*, Lake Oswego Oregon, Metamorphous Press, 1982

Quilliam, Susan. *The Eternal Triangle*, London, Pan Books, 1990

Quilliam, Susan and Grove-Stephensen, Ian. *How to Stay in Love*, Milton Keynes, Helpful Books, 1988

Stanway, Dr Andrew. *The Joy of Sexual Fantasy*, London, Headline, 1991

Contact Organizations

These organizations provide help and support for a variety of sexual and relationship issues.

American Association of Marriage and Family Therapy, 1100 17th Street, N.W., 10th Floor, Washington, D.C. 20036. (202) 452-0109

The American Association of Sex Educators, Counselors and Therapists (AASECT), 435 North Michigan Avenue, Suite 1717, Chicago, IL 60611. (312) 644-0828

Association of Couples for Marriage Enrichment, Inc., P.O. Box 10596, Winston-Salem, N.C. 27108. (919) 724-1526

Institute of Marriage and Family Relations, 6116 Rolling Road, Suite 316, Springfield, VA 22152. (703) 569-2400

Masters and Johnson Institute, 24 South Kingshighway, St. Louis, MO 63108. (314) 361-2377

National Council on Family Relations, 3989 Central Avenue, N.E., Suite 550, Minneapolis, MN 55421. (612) 781-9331

Planned Parenthood ® Federation of America, Inc., 810 Seventh Avenue, New York, NY 10019. (212) 541-7800

The Society for the Scientific Study of Sex, Inc. (SSSS), P.O. Box 208, Mount Vernon, IA 52314. (319) 895-8407

INDEX

ACKNOWLEDGEMENTS

I would like to thank everyone who has helped me with this book, particularly Alan, Dee, Helen, Leafy, Lynne, Peter and all the other anonymous people who shared with me their experiences of love-making. My thanks to my agent Barbara Levy, and to Nick Eddison, Ian Jackson, Michele Doyle, Hilary Krag and everyone at Eddison Sadd, for making the preparation of the book such a truly enjoyable and educational experience. Thanks too to Harold Harris and all the models and make-up artists, for teaching me how much hard work goes into creating the photographs. Finally to my partner Ian, without whom I never would have discovered sexual body talk.

Editor Michele Doyle
Designer Hilary Krag
Illustrator Anthony Duke
Picture Researcher Liz Eddison
Indexer Michael Allaby
Proofreaders Fiona Eves and Chris Norris
Production Hazel Kirkman and Charles James
Creative Director Nick Eddison
Editorial Director Ian Jackson

Eddison Sadd would like to acknowledge the following, who gave permission to reproduce the illustrations:

t = top; b = below; c = centre; l = left; r = right

David De Lossey/The Image Bank 24/25c, 101tl; Larry Dale Gordon/The Image Bank 15; The Hutchison Library 17tr, 20, 26/27, 97; Steve Niedorf/The Image Bank 108; NZS Ent, Inc/The Image Bank 111; Michael Salas/The Image Bank 33l; G & J M Stane/The Image Bank 5; Picturebank Photo Library 61l; ZEFA 2, 6, 9, 10b, 11tr,tl,b, 12, 17tl,tc,cl,bl,br, 18, 19, 21, 23, 24l, 25tr,cr,br, 28, 29l,r, 30, 31, 32, 33r, 34l,r, 37t,c,b, 38, 40, 41tr,tl,br, 43, 44, 45, 47, 48/49, 50, 51, 52, 53tl,tr,c,b, 55, 56, 57t,bl,br, 58t,b, 59l,r, 60, 61r, 63, 64, 65tr,tl,br,bl, 67l,r, 68, 71, 73, 74/75, 77, 78t,b, 79, 80t,bl,br, 82/83, 85tl,tc,tr,b, 87t,c,bl,bc,br, 88, 90l,c,r, 91t,b, 92/93, 94, 95, 98, 99tl,tr,bl,bc,br, 101tr,br, 103, 105, 106, 107, 113tl,tr,cr,bl,bc, 115, 117tr,tl,b, 119l,r, 120, 123

Front Jacket : ZEFA
Back Jacket : Larry Dale Gordon/The Image Bank